Competitive
Bidding

Other books by Jeremy Flint

Why You Lose at Racing (with Freddie North)
Trick 13 (with Terence Reese)
Instructions for the Defence (with David Greenwood)
Tiger Bridge (with Freddie North)
Bridge: The Golden Principles (with Freddie North)
Bridge: The First Principles (with Freddie North)
Bridge in the Looking Glass (with Freddie North)
The First Bridge Book (with John Gullick)
Bridge with the Times
The Winning Edge

By Richard Sharp

The Game of Diplomacy

Competitive Bidding

Jeremy Flint and
Richard Sharp

ROBERT HALE · LONDON

Copyright © Jeremy Flint and Richard Sharp 1980
First published 1980
This edition 1987

ISBN 0 7090 2929 2

Robert Hale Limited
Clerkenwell House
Clerkenwell Green
London EC1R 0HT

Printed in Great Britain by
St Edmundsbury Press Limited, Bury St Edmunds, Suffolk
Bound by WBC Bookbinders

Contents

1. Overcalls

In the old days the experts, almost as a matter of pride, took care to keep their overcalls up to strength. The side which held the balance of power performed a graceful pas de deux while the opponents maintained a respectful silence. The Italian Blue team changed all that, constantly introducing featherweight overcalls and 'unsound' take-out doubles. The conservative experts shook their heads and foretold instant doom, but twenty years later these light overcalls and aggressive interventions have earned almost universal acceptance.

It pays to get into the bidding. Most non-expert partnerships will bid considerably less accurately if there has been even one intervening bid from the opposition: mistakes of valuation creep in, doubts arise about whether sequences are forcing or not, and often no one gets round to bidding a sound no-trump contract because neither partner is sufficiently happy with his holding in the opponents' suit. Of all the oars you can stick in, a simple overcall muddies the water most effectively.

Consider the following four hands: in each case you are South, the vulnerability is in your favour, and East has dealt and opened 1♣ in front of you.

(a) ♠AQJ75 (b) ♠AKQ10 (c) ♠AQJ76 (d) ♠AQJ84
    ♡942   ♡976   ♡K94   ♡K93
    ◇65   ◇832   ◇Q2   ◇A7
    ♣873   ♣875   ♣653   ♣984

With each of these hands you should make your presence felt with an overcall of 1♠. With hand (a), your objective is simply to make a nuisance of yourself, and you will often achieve this modest aim – if West is sitting over you with some such holding as ♠64, ♡QJ53, ◇A1094, ♣542 your overcall will certainly inconvenience him, and unless he is playing some form of negative double it will probably silence him altogether. At the prevailing vulnerability it is unlikely that you will be doubled for penalties, and the reasons for bidding far outweigh the possible risks: you have secured a promising lead should West become declarer, you have prevented him from bidding either red suit at a convenient level, and if East–West are really strong you may have talked them out of a no-trump contract into an inferior suit game.

This last argument is the reason for making an unorthodox 1♠ overcall on hand (b). Clearly neither opponent will have a reliable-looking spade stop, and both will now have reason to suspect that you can run at least five spade tricks against a no-trump contract. An overcall on a 4-card suit is not often sound, but here the slight risk is more than justified.

Hand (c) is a minimum opening bid, and now you are interested in contesting the part-score. If partner raises to 2♠ you will probably make it, though a more likely outcome is that you will push your opponents to the 3-level, where their contract will be harder to land. Game for your side is certainly not out of the question, but investigating this is not your principal purpose in bidding.

Hand (d) is about a maximum for the simple overcall at this vulnerability. With sound opening values and a good suit, you cannot dismiss prospects of game facing a partner who has not yet had a chance to express an opinion. If he makes any kind of encouraging overture you will be able to accept his suggestion, conscious that you have values to spare for your first bid.

In the examples given above, vulnerability was in your favour, and your suit was good. These are the two all-important factors when considering whether or not your hand justifies a simple overcall. At equal vulnerability, opponents will certainly consider the possibility of a penalty double; and if you are a game up they will be positively trigger-happy. As for the suit quality, we can do no better than repeat the old adage: an opening bid shows a good *hand*, but an overcall – and especially a 2-level overcall – shows a good *suit*.

No overcall is ever free of some element of risk. What you

must consider is whether the tactical advantages justify that risk. In the examples given, conditions were as favourable as they can be: the opponents only were vulnerable, your suit was spades (guaranteeing that you can overcall at the 1-level), and the opening bid was 1♣, so that the spade overcall would have the maximum possible pre-emptive effect.

In such conditions, all you need is a good suit and an aggressive instinct.

It is possible to lay down a few rules governing the simple overcall. Like all rules, they exist to be broken . . . but they will at least warn you when you are about to stick your neck out too far.

1) In principle, any overcall shows a 5-card or longer suit; 4-card suits should be introduced only rarely, and with careful forethought. We have seen one instance already in hand (b) above – here is another.

♠AKJ7 ♡94 ◇Q876 ♣K32

This hand justifies a minimum take-out double of a 1♡ opening, but it is unsuitable for a double of 1♣ or 1◇ because of the bad hearts. Over an opening 1♣, a 1♠ overcall is worth risking at any vulnerability, despite the 4-card suit – you cut out a 1♡ response, you indicate a good lead, and your spades are strong enough to suggest that a penalty double may not be easy to find. Over 1◇, the decision is more difficult; you have some defence to a diamond contract, which suggests that the opener's partner may be short in diamonds, and thus more inclined to double you. If vulnerable you should pass – if not, the risk is worth while. Still, you should bear in mind that your partner will expect a 5-card suit, and you should not disappoint him too often.

2) When you are vulnerable, your opponents will be alert for a lucrative penalty double. With fairly even distribution and the certainty that his side has the balance of the high cards, your left-hand opponent will be keen to double for a safe plus score rather than stretch for the doubtful game. The better your suit, the less likely you are to be doubled; and the axe is far less prone to fall at the 1-level than at the 2-level. So a vulnerable overcall should be based on a good 5-card suit, or if at the 2-level on a

good 6-card suit. When you introduce a 4-card suit, as in the example above, you should be conscious that you are taking your life in your hands, and you should be ready with a comprehensive set of excuses.

3) The maximum point-count for a simple overcall is around 15 – a little less with a fair 6-card suit. To make the bid with better hands puts an unreasonable strain on partner. As it is, he will have difficulty allowing for the very wide range of the overcall. With an overcall bordering on the maximum range, it is wiser, if in doubt, to start with a take-out double.

4) It is best to avoid overcalling on a poor suit. With a hand such as this:

♠J8753 ♡AQ9 ◇KJ7 ♣J2

after an opening bid of 1♣, 1◇ or 1♡ on your right it is tempting to overcall 1♠, which is what you would have opened, after all. But the drawbacks are very real: your opponents may well have good enough spades to judge when a double will be a sound investment, and if you eventually end up defending the hand you will have a nasty moment when your partner kicks off with ♠K from Kx. There will be little harm done if you make a take-out double of 1♣ on this hand, while over 1◇ or 1♡ it will usually pay to make a cowardly pass. After all, opening bids of one of a suit are rarely passed out; you should get a second chance to bid.

5) The more bidding space your overcall consumes, the better excuse there is for making it. Reverting to our first example, we advocated a 1♠ overcall over 1♣ on this meagre collection:

♠AQJ75 ♡942 ◇65 ♣873

The most important argument in favour of this bid is that it shuts out a 1-level response in either red suit. Suppose instead that the opening bid is 1♡. In this case a 1♠ overcall not only fails to hinder the next player but may actively assist him. The only bid you have shut out is a response of 1♠, and if that is what he was going to bid you would prefer to hear about it before committing yourself. In the meantime you have enriched his bidding vocabulary to the extent of a double, and you may have also given him the option of passing on a borderline responding hand with no fit for his partner, such as this:

♠8 ♡73 ◇Q8742 ♣KJ652

where, but for your intervention, he would have had to bid an extremely reluctant 1NT. Spades may still be a good lead, but other than that the tactical advantages of bidding are non-existent, and a disciplined player will pass.

We must now move on to consider the situation that arises when your right-hand opponent has opened with something other than a natural bid of one of a suit.

In the duplicate game, it is increasingly likely nowadays that an opening 1♣ will be artificial and forcing, showing at least 16 or 17 points (depending on the system) and a completely unspecified distribution. The most effective counter to this artificial bid is to reduce the minimum requirements for your overcalls. Your opponents will rarely be able to double with confidence – a double on the first round is usually conventional, and in any case neither player will have much idea of the nature of his partner's hand. As against this, the best action with a strong hand is usually a pass; you know you will get another chance, as the 1♣ bidder will certainly speak again, and after you have heard three bids from your opponents you may well be congratulating yourself on your apparent timidity. This hand from a recent duplicate pairs is a typical case:

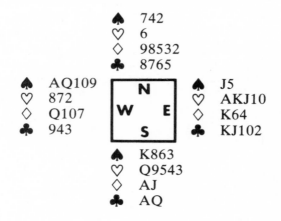

North dealt at Game All. Where East opened a natural 1♣, South made the obvious take-out double, and some Wests bid 1NT. When East now made a sensible pass (if West had enough for game to be a good bet he should have redoubled in the first place) some Souths chanced a penalty double, and East came out of the bushes with a smart redouble. Whatever evasive tactics North–South tried proved unavailing, and plus scores of 800 or more to East–West were common.

At several tables East opened with a Precision 1♣, and where South came in on the first round he met with a similar fate to those Souths countering a natural 1♣. At one table South found the recommended pass, and West bid 1♠, showing a moderate hand with balanced distribution. When East rebid 1NT South was able to place his partner with precisely nothing, and was not tempted to enter the fray. The defence was difficult, but a score of —150 was above average for North–South.

Another artificial opening which should be briefly mentioned is the Precision 1♢, which though not forcing may be made by some partnerships with a doubleton in the suit. The only special principle to be considered here is what the overcaller should do when he holds a diamond suit, and we shall examine this point when discussing cue-bids of the opponents' suit later.

The other common type of opening bid – excluding pre-emptive calls of various kinds, which will be treated separately – is 1NT. Particular caution is needed when competing over this opening – its considerable pre-emptive effect means that the overcaller will have to say his piece at an inconvenient level. A particular advantage of the weak 1NT is that the opener's partner will be very well placed to make a penalty double, knowing his partner's strength and shape so precisely. It is certainly wise to use some form of conventional defence to this opening (some of the possible choices are considered in Chapter 5); natural overcalls on one-suited hands should be well up to standard in suit quality and general strength. When in doubt, stay out of the auction, at least for the first round, and hope that your good suit will be useful in defence. Suppose for instance that with your side vulnerable you hold this hand:

♠Q86   ♡QJ5   ◇J2   ♣AKJ96

after a 1NT opening on your right. Even if your methods allow a natural 2♣ overcall, nothing could be more futile than such a bid here. You have not used up any bidding space; you have told the enemy which suit they have to fear at no trumps; your outside values may tell in defence but will be useless in a club contract; and you cannot even claim to be showing a good lead, as if you pass it will be your lead anyway! This is a classic example of a purposeless overcall. Always ask yourself what your overcall will achieve, and if you receive an unfavourable reply then have the discipline to pass.

We can conclude this section on the simple overcall by examining the case where the overcaller has previously passed. An extraordinary number of players cling to the obviously illogical notion that it is safer to bid on the second round than on the first. West on the following hand was one of this breed, and North-South were quick to profit from his delusion.

Dealer West, Game All

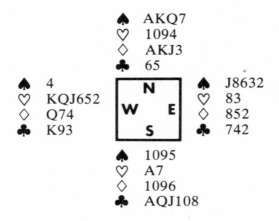

```
                    ♠ AKQ7
                    ♡ 1094
                    ◇ AKJ3
                    ♣ 65
         ♠ 4            N            ♠ J8632
         ♡ KQJ652                    ♡ 83
         ◇ Q74       W     E         ◇ 852
         ♣ K93          S            ♣ 742
                    ♠ 1095
                    ♡ A7
                    ◇ 1096
                    ♣ AQJ108
```

After West had cautiously passed as dealer, North opened 1♠ and South replied 2♣. Before North could decide whether to risk a shot at 3NT despite the wide-open hearts, West came to the rescue by bidding 2♡, which North gratefully doubled. Good defence netted an 800 penalty, more than adequate compensation for missing the shaky 3NT contract, which makes only because of the fortunate lie of the diamonds. The principle involved here, of course, is that an overcall which would be risky anyway becomes doubly so once you have announced that you were too weak to open the bidding. This is not to say that it is never sound to overcall after passing; but a vulnerable intervention at the 2-level when both opponents are unlimited is simply asking for trouble.

Jump Overcalls
In standard British bidding methods a jump overcall shows a good 6-card or longer suit and at least the values for a non-minimum opening bid. The jump overcall is strictly non-forcing, and a hand good enough for an Acol Two is too strong for the bid and should be introduced with a take-out double. The minimum range can be shaded slightly, depending on the vulnerability, and on the level at which the bid must be made.

	(a)	(b)	(c)
♠	9	AKJ875	2
♡	AQJ764	A9	J84
◇	A83	KJ9	AJ2
♣	K62	64	AKQJ95

Hand (a) is worth 2♡ over one of a minor at any vulnerability, though if vulnerable it is a minimum for the bid. Not vulnerable one would also bid 3♡ over 1♠, but if vulnerable 2♡ would be enough, as this is in any case a fairly strong bid. One of the advantages of the jump over the minor opening is that it may shut out the spade suit; it is the loss of this bonus, plus the extra risk involved in venturing to the 3-level, that makes 3♡ over 1♠ a doubtful proposition.

Hand (b) is a maximum for a non-vulnerable 2♠ overcall – with another queen it would be too good, though if the opening bid was one of a minor you might still consider bidding 2♠ for tactical reasons, rather than the technically correct take-out double, which might allow opponents to find a heart fit.

Hand (c) is worth a jump overcall in clubs at any vulnerability. Minor-suit jump overcalls are usually aiming for 3NT, and it is particularly important to keep the quality of the suit up to scratch – with more than one loser in the long suit it is wiser to look for some alternative bid.

An occasional source of disagreement is whether the jump

overcaller should be allowed a second suit. This hand caused difficulties in a major pairs tournament during 1979:

♠AQ76   ♡9   ◇AKJ843   ♣75

At Game All, after an opening 1♣ on the right, some players elected to bid 2◇ on these cards while others, with an eye to a possible spade fit, preferred a take-out double. The doublers ran into trouble when partner, holding:

♠9   ♡A108642   ◇Q65   ♣A92

quite reasonably jumped straight to 4♡, after which several pairs incurred minus scores, and none bid the moderately good slam. After the 2◇ overcall the bidding proceeded smoothly enough by way of a forcing 2♡ response and a 2♠ rebid, after which most players reached either the cold 3NT or the border-line but makable 6◇. It is of course possible to construct hands where the double would have worked better, but on the whole it seems wise to stick to the principle that two-suited hands, even of the 6-4 type, should not be entrusted to the overworked take-out double, especially if short in either major.

Higher jump overcalls are natural and pre-emptive, and the minimum requirements should be set rather higher than for an opening pre-empt, as the risk is much greater while much of the advantage has been lost now that the opponents have opened.

In some countries, most notably the United States, it is standard to play all jump overcalls as weak. Thus a bid of, say, 2♠ over 1◇ describes a hand similar to an opening Weak Two, with roughly 6-11 high-card points and a 6-card or very good 5-card suit. Although this method is less frequently used in Britain, there are two cases in which it is worth while for any pair to play weak jump overcalls. One is when the overcaller has previously passed, though this is open to the objections noted earlier. The more important instance is when an opponent has opened with an artificial 1♣. We have already said that the best way to handle a strong hand in this situation is to pass and await developments, so the jump overcall can be reserved for weak hands with a good suit. The same principle can be applied (with a little more circumspection) by fourth hand after the bidding has started 1♣-No-1◇. This type of bid does undoubtedly cause the 1♣ opening to lose some of its accuracy – the 1♣

systems are seen at their best when the strong opening is followed by an uncontested auction, and any spanner that can be thrown in at this early stage is well worth throwing.

The 1NT Overcall

Unless it is ascribed a conventional meaning, the overcall of 1NT is always a strong bid, irrespective of the type of opening 1NT in use. The most popular range is 15-17, though some partnerships prefer a point stronger. The hand need not be entirely balanced – indeed, a 1NT overcall is sometimes a good gambit on quite distributional hands, perhaps containing a singleton or a 6-card suit. In theory the 1NT bidder promises a double stop in the suit bid against him; in practice it may be wise to bend this rule slightly if the choice is between 1NT and a trap pass.

	(a)		(b)		(c)
	♠K6		♠AQ7		♠KQ7
	♡AQ74		♡9		♡AQ9
	♢A103		♢KQ65		♢A107532
	♣K1072		♣AJ842		♣2

Hand (a) is a routine 1NT overcall of a 1♣ or 1♡ opening on your right. Over 1♠ it is certainly better to make a take-out double, with a tenuous spade guard and four good cards in the unbid major. Over 1♢ the decision is closer, but 1NT is clearly preferable – it only needs partner to hold Jx to give you a second stop, and a take-out double is always unattractive with a doubleton spade and no 5-card suit.

Hand (b) has an obvious take-out double of 1♡, while over 1♣ there is no sensible alternative to a trap pass. Most players would also pass over 1♢, though there is something to be said for the tactical underbid of 2♣, shutting out a 1♡ response. Over 1♠, the most effective move is to bid 1NT – if partner bids large numbers of hearts you will just have to pretend that you misheard the bidding, and that your 1NT was intended as 'Unusual'.

Hand (c) is one that most players would mismanage at the table. Whatever the opening bid, a simple overcall in diamonds grossly undervalues a 5-loser hand, while a jump overcall on such a thin minor suit is equally misleading. Over a 1♣ opening it is best to double, but if the opener has bid either major 1NT is the most practical bid.

Because 1 NT is always a dangerous overcall, exposed as it is to an easy penalty double by third hand, various conventional uses have been devised for it over the years. In the obsolete Baron System it was used as a weak take-out double, an idea which surprisingly survives today among the few players of 'Baronized Acol'; the obvious objection is that the announcement of weakness makes it easy for the opener's side to decide what to do. 1NT may also be treated as 'Unusual' in some situations, and we shall examine this convention later.

Perhaps the most interesting of the conventional uses of 1NT is the Gardener or 'Comic' variety, where the overcall may be normal or may be an assortment of rubbish with a long suit. This enjoyable gadget is not licensed for use in English Bridge Union competitions, but many top players favour it, and it has proved very effective against weak opposition, where there may be interesting partnership misunderstandings about which sequences are forcing and how to proceed with very distributional hands. Consider: your partner opens 1♡, next hand overcalls 1NT, announced as 'Comic', and you hold one of these hands:

(a)	♠AQJ76	(b) ♠AQJ76
	♡7	♡AQ942
	◇4	◇–
	♣AK10965	♣J65

You know that the 1NT bid is a nonsense, but how do you tell your partner? In fact the obviously correct first move on both hands is to bid 2NT . . . but not everyone will think of it at the time.

One final point about the 1NT overcall is that it is a favourite vehicle for the psychic bidder. Because a psychic 1NT overcall is a gross mis-statement of values it should be possible to spot it and deal with it more easily than other psychs, but in practice it produces frequent successes against weak or even moderate opposition. As with the Gardener convention, the essential thing for the opponents is to unmask the deception as quickly as possible with a 2NT bid on distributional hands or a penalty double where you are sure you are not missing anything better.

Of the remaining no-trump overcalls, a jump to 2NT is almost always played as 'Unusual' and will be discussed later. A direct 3NT is a rare but useful bid, showing a goodish hand with a very strong suit and a trick in the suit bid by the opponents. Over an opening 1♠, bid 3NT on:

♠AQ   ♡J73   ◇AKQ9542   ♣6

If the opponents ingenuously lead a spade you should have your nine tricks; if they have played before they will no doubt lead something else, but you need little from partner to bring in your contract. It is expedient to play this bid as showing, in principle, no sure trick outside your long suit and the opponents' suit – this allows the overcaller to leave rescue operations to his partner, and to take full advantage of the unwise doubles this bid often provokes.

2. Bidding after an overcall

Any kind of overcall by the player sitting over the opening bidder provides problems for everyone at the table. The auction will not now develop (in most cases) along standard approach-forcing lines, and tactical considerations become at least as important as the search for accuracy and definition. Much of the best modern bidding theory has gone into improving the ways in which both sides can cope with the contested auction: the main fruits of this research so far have been the Sputnik Double and the Competitive Double, two vital new weapons which will each have a chapter to themselves later in this book; and the Unassuming Cue Bid, covered in this chapter. But first, we examine the routine ways in which casual partnerships should develop their hands in the contested auction.

A. THE OPENER'S PARTNER

The position of the opener's partner is likely to get worse rather than better when an overcall is made on his right. True, his bidding vocabulary has been extended by two new possibilities – a double (which we assume for the present is for penalties), and a cue-bid in opponents' suit. He also has the option of passing gratefully on hands where without the overcall he would have bid with reluctance. On the other hand there are many run-of-the-mill holdings he may have where he knows he should bid something yet nothing sensible suggests itself.

(a)	♠KJ7	(b) ♠85	(c) ♠874
	♡J875	♡Q63	♡QJ9
	♢943	♢J5	♢KQ32
	♣K72	♣K107643	♣AQ6

These three hands show the more favourable aspect of the position. After 1♢ from partner and a 1♠ overcall on your right, you are at least as well placed as you would have ben without the intervention. On hand (a) you wanted to bid 1NT but felt perhaps that you ought to bid the horrible heart suit – well, now you can bid 1NT with a clear conscience, telling partner at once about the balanced shape, modest point-count and good values in spades. The 1NT response should of course be full value after the overcall, roughly 8-10 points, so this hand is about minimum for the bid.

On hand (b) you were going to bid a dutiful but horrible 1NT, which you would certainly not have enjoyed playing if partner had passed it. Now you can leave it to him, with an (inaudible) sigh of relief. With luck you may even get a chance to bid your clubs at the 2-level on the next round, which you would certainly not have been able to do without the overcall.

Hand (c) is a rather different sort of problem. Without the overcall your only possible choices would have been a wild bash at 3NT or a rather uneasy 2♣, which would probably have worked all right but might have left you in an awkward spot if partner had rebid 2♢. Now you can describe your hand very well with a cue-bid of 2♠, which your partner should initially read as showing game values but no stop in spades. If partner rebids 2NT you raise to 3NT; if not, then 3NT is probably not playable and you will have to consider alternatives. The overcall here may well have helped to keep you out of an unmakable game.

The next three hands show the other side of the coin:

(d) ♠74   (e) ♠765   (f) ♠72
     ♡KJ65   ♡KJ76   ♡KQJ865
     ♢Q832   ♢A843   ♢108
     ♣J73   ♣Q9   ♣964

After 1♣ from partner and 1♠ on your right, all these everday holdings have suddenly become almost unbiddable. With hand (d) you cannot really bid anything except 2♣, a bid which hardly describes the hand well – a forcing response in a red suit is out of the question on such a poor hand, so the only alternative is a pass, which makes little appeal. On hand (e) you must grit your teeth and bid 2♢, which may pass off all right, but may also produce an appalling result if partner has:

♠Q83   ♡92   ♢K76   ♣AK754

Whichever form of suicide your partner now selects, it will be painful. As for hand (f), the only rational course of action is to pass, in the faint hope that you may get a chance to show the hearts next time. It is because common hands like these led to such idiotic results that the Sputnik Double was devised – this admirable convention will get you out of trouble on (d) and (e), while its spin-off benefit, the non-forcing free bid, will handle (f) for you.

To summarize the options open to third hand after a simple suit overcall, most bids retain their normal meaning. 1NT is now a little stronger than the polite courtesy response in the uncontested auction, and guarantees a holding in opponents' suit. Raises are normal, except that single raises may have to be made on 3-card support, even in a minor suit. A double is for penalties in standard methods, and this will be covered in another chapter. The cue-bid of opponents' suit is assumed to be based on a no-trump type of hand with game values and no guard in opponents' suit, but may also be used on other game-going hands with no better bid available. For instance, after 1♡ from partner and 2♣ on your right, you hold:

♠AQ76   ♡KQ86   ♢K95   ♣A10

Some players would see this as the moment to plunge uninhibitedly into Blackwood, or put partner on the rack with a force of 3♠, but the best course of action for the present is to establish a game-forcing situation with 3♣ and see what happens next.

Th 1NT overcall introduces several new ideas for third hand. For a start, this is the one situation in which it is standard to play a free bid in a new suit as non-forcing – in the sequence 1♠-1NT-2♢, responder shows a good diamond suit, usually of at least 6 cards, and not enough ammunition to venture a penalty double. Jump bids in new suits are traditionally pre-emptive, though this gambit is attended by obvious risks and should be used sparingly. Indeed, with the increasing use of psychic and 'comic' 1NT overcalls, it is wiser to use the jump in a new suit as a natural force, based on a strong one-suited hand, or a good suit and a 4-card fit for opener. With most moderate to strong hands it is correct to double, which is strictly for penalties and shows 9 points upwards – a common mistake is to raise the opening bid on fairly balanced hands with modest trump support, which usually results in exchanging a large plus score for a larger minus. Raises should be made on distributional hands with little defence.

There are two special problems which arise with the 1NT overcall. The more common occurs when the 1NT bidder is not vulnerable and his opponents are: there is now a considerable temptation for third hand (holding, say, a balanced 9-count) to say to himself, 'I know I can probably beat 1NT if I double it, but if we have game on our way I may not get a big enough penalty.' This is reasonable as far as it goes, but the important thing to remember is that partner too knows the score (we hope), and if you make your natural double he is free to remove it if he thinks the vulnerable game is on. A useful expert understanding covers this situation – the double of a 1NT overcall at unfavourable vulnerability is limited to 9-11 points, so that the doubling side can judge correctly to accept a penalty only when there is no likelihood of game.

The other catch has already been referred to, and is exemplified by this hand from a team-of-four match. At Love All you hold:

♠AQ764 ♡K95 ♢– ♣AJ863

and the bidding surprisingly starts with 1♡ from your partner and 1NT on your right. Clearly the overcaller is pulling your leg, and you may be tempted to teach him a lesson by doubling – if he escapes into his long diamond suit you can cue-bid diamonds yourself, and an elegant sequence will take you to the best slam. So reasoned the player who held this hand . . . but alas, the 1NT bidder not only stood the double but made his contract in some comfort for an enormous swing – his hand was:

♠85 ♡A6 ♢AKQ1043 ♣952

and he had the good fortune to find the ♢J in dummy! It was of course naive to lead a heart after this bidding, but even a black suit lead would have produced only 700, a poor result for the defenders as they can make a slam in any of three suits. The answer of course is that you should bid 2NT at your first turn, showing a strong distributional hand unsuited to defence, which makes the slam easy to reach.

Higher Overcalls

Strong jump overcalls are best handled by the Sputnik Double – it is especially futile to play penalty doubles in this situation. Pre-emptive jumps of various kinds are intended to cause third hand acute difficulty, and often do. No sophisticated weaponry exists to deal with these tactics: all one can say is that you should be reluctant to pass, and if in doubt you should settle for a penalty double; it may be galling to be bounced out of a game for a miserable 100 or 300, but it is infinitely worse to end up losing points in a silly high-level contract. Every now and then the double will misfire, and you will have to endure listening to your opponents' telling you that you could have made eleven tricks in clubs instead of letting them make 4♠ doubled; but it is best to become known as a doubler in these positions, so that opponents will think twice before taking too many liberties at your table.

B. THE OVERCALLER'S PARTNER

Responding to overcalls is a completely different matter to responding to opening bids. Forget all about point-counts, carefully defined limit-bids and approach-forcing manoeuvres: after your partner has overcalled you are likely only to get one bid, and you should look for the one which will be most helpful to your partner and most embarrassing to your opponents.

(i) Simple Change of Suit

An immediate difference – a change of suit facing an overcall is not forcing. It is mildly constructive, but suggests a dislike for partner's suit.

	(a)	(b)	(c)
	♠J75	♠8	♠1087
	♡83	♡J93	♡2
	◇AQ64	◇AK8763	◇AQ9864
	♣K1053	♣Q54	♣653

It is of interest to consider these three hands in the light of several different overcalling sequences. First, suppose that 1♡ has been opened on your left (at equal vulnerability), partner has overcalled 1♠, and next hand has passed. On hand (a) you should not even consider any action other than raising the spades – 2♠ is enough for the present, though you can push on to 3♠ in competition. (This hand is also suitable for the Unassuming Cue-Bid, described later.) Hand (b) is the type on which you should bid 2◇, showing fair values but dislike of your partner's spades. Hand (c) is more of a problem – it is surprising that there has been a pass on your right, and left-hand opponent probably has a big hand. There is something to be said for bidding a misleading 2◇ now, confident that you will get a chance to raise spades on the next round, but it is more sensible to support the spades at once, giving opener less room to describe his powerful hand.

Now let us consider the situation in reverse, with 1♠ as the opening bid and 2♡ as your partner's overcall. With hand (a) you should certainly allow partner to play in hearts, as his 2-level overcall guarantees a good suit – a pass is correct if not vulnerable, but if he has made a vulnerable 2-level overcall you cannot rule out game, and should make a further move. With hand (b) you should go straight to 4♡ at any vulnerability, without any thought of introducing the diamonds. On hand (c) it would be criminal to 'rescue' partner into diamonds, yet many players would do so. The bid merely increases the chances of incurring a penalty double, with no real reason to expect you will improve the contract.

For our last example, let us assume that the bidding has started with 1♠ on your left, 2♡ from partner and 2♠ on your right. The spade support has slightly improved hand (a), as the knowledge that your partner is likely to be short in spades means that your minor-suit honours should pull their weight. You are worth 4♡ now – true, you may not make it, but opponents are quite likely to misjudge the position and soldier on to 4♠, which you are probably going to defeat.

Hand (b) has not been improved by the spade raise – you already knew you were short in the suit, and now it seems very likely that opponents will go to 4♠ over 4♡, giving you one of those unpleasant high-level decisions you always get wrong. The best move here is to bid 3◇: while it is true that this is non-forcing it is most unlikely to become the final contract, since partner will place you with some support for his good heart suit. (With no fit for hearts, of course, you would be happy to pass here.) The reason for bidding 3◇ is that you tell partner where your defensive tricks are, making it easier for him to judge what to do over 4♠. Here are two possible hands he may hold:

(d) ♠K72		(e) ♠QJ7	
♡AQ10864		♡108754	
◇5		◇Q52	
♣J63		♣A	
1♠	2♡	2♠	3◇
No	3♡	3♠	4♡
4♠	?		

With hand (d) the misfit in diamonds is a clear pointer that a double is best, but with (e), despite the superficially better defensive values, it is easy to see that one should press on with 5♡ – not 5◇, as this will help opponents to judge that the time has come to sacrifice.

Reverting to the original sequence 1♠-2♡-2♠, with hand (c) it is of course correct to pass, hoping to defeat 4♠ with a heart ruff or two, and delighted meanwhile to be out of the firing-line

(ii) Jump Change of Suit
A jump in a new suit facing an overcall is forcing, and shows a good 6-card suit. There is little that needs to be added to that, except to say that the overcaller should look for something more helpful to say than simply rebidding his known long suit.

(a) ♠AQ9632	(b) ♠AQ853	(c) ♠AQ853
♡Q76	♡6	♡KJ7
◇7	◇Q87	◇108
♣K105	♣A932	♣Q95

Consider your action with each of these hands after the bidding:

1♡	1♠	No	3◇
No	?		

With hand (a) the best bid is 3♡, the enemy suit, hoping that your partner will be able to show some sort of spade support, or even bid 3NT. Hand (b) has become a whale after this bidding, and no straightforward diamond raise does justice to it – the best move is an advance cue-bid of 4♣, intending to follow with 4♡ if partner rebids his diamonds. With hand (c) you should show the good heart values by bidding 3NT, which should play well if your partner is trusting enough to pass it.

How far this jump shift should be forcing is a matter for partnership agreement. With overcalls tending to be so fragile nowadays it is perhaps impractical to play it as unconditionally forcing to game, and the best answer may be to regard it as forcing to suit-agreement, so that (in the examples above) a simple raise to 4◇ by the overcaller could be passed.

(iii) Raises and the Unassuming Cue-Bid

As we have already seen, very little in the way of trump support is needed to raise an overcall. Three-card support is always enough, and if the overcall was made at the 2-level you can raise cheerfully with a doubleton, or even a singleton honour:

♠842 ♡AK76 ◇AK95 ♣J3

With your side only vulnerable, the bidding goes 1♠ on your left, 2♣ from partner, 3♠ on your right. What now? If you slipped this hand into the average club pairs evening the traveller at the end would show a plethora of 3♠ doubled and made ('I have four tricks and surely partner can contribute one'), with the occasional 3NT —1 ('Partner must have *something* outside clubs, so I'll hope it's in spades'). Some pairs will no doubt push their opponents into 4♠, which should at least produce a small plus score. You may be outraged by the suggestion that the proper bid in the sequence given is 5♣ . . . but can you construct a hand for partner that will not offer a play for it, given that he is unlikely to hold more than one spade? We would seriously be more afraid of missing 6♣ than of being defeated in 5♣. What is more, we would still make the same bid if the small club was a small diamond!

One frequent problem that used to arise has been largely solved by the many converts to a useful modern gadget, the Unassuming Cue-Bid.

(a) ♠KJ95
    ♡8
    ◇Q7642
    ♣762

(b) ♠KJ95
    ♡82
    ◇AQ7
    ♣QJ94

After 1♡ on your left, 1♠ from partner and 2♣ on your right, you would like to raise to 3♠ on both these hands, for different reasons. With hand (a) you feel reasonably sure that the enemy can make 4♡, and your object is to make it more difficult for them to bid it. Hand (b) is a different case, affording high hopes of game though not strong enough to bid 4♠ direct facing the sort of rubbish that sometimes makes up a 1-level overcall. But if you bid 3♠ on both these hands, what is partner supposed to do holding:

♠AQ764 ♡953 ◇K83 ♣K5

which produces an easy game opposite hand (b) but almost no play for one facing (a)?

The Unassuming Cue-Bid solves this problem. Under this arrangement, a bid of opponents' suit by the overcaller's partner in the first instance promises the values for a sound raise, but if followed by a further display of strength is invitational to game. The cue-bidder may be intending to support his partner's suit, or may be looking for game in some other strain. Thus in the situation given, with hand (a) make a pre-emptive raise to 3♠, but with (b) bid 2♡, the enemy suit, and support spades on the next round.

This device has several advantages. Not only does it enable the overcaller to judge when to try for game, it also helps him decide whether or not to sacrifice if the opposition push on – the message of a U.C.B. followed by a raise is that the hand contains defensive tricks. It follows that you should be sparing with your penalty doubles after a normal jump raise in competition.

After the U.C.B., the overcaller should again try to find some more helpful move than a simple rebid of his original suit. Reverting to the example hands on p. 19, we will now assume that the bidding has gone 1♡ on your right, 1♠ from you, No Bid on your left, 2♡ (U.C.B.) from partner, No Bid on your right. With hand (a) you should bid 3♠, stressing the good

6-card suit and the non-minimum values. With hand (b) introduce your second suit with 3♣, effectively forcing, and make a further bid on the next round. On hand (c) you should bid 2NT now and pass a non-forcing return to 3♠ – your heart values are probably wasted in a spade contract, and the hand is unlikely to play well.

A final point of interest about the U.C.B. is what happens when opponents have bid two suits. Our suggestion here is that the bid should always be made in the opener's suit, which must be the lower of the two possibilities; a bid of responder's suit is thus a normal cue-bid, agreeing overcaller's suit and showing a control.

(iv) No-Trump Bids

No-trump bids by the overcaller's partner are completely natural, guaranteeing adequate holdings in any suits bid by opener's side. The main point to remember here is that any no-trump bid should allow for the fact that overcaller may be quite weak in high cards and should therefore be considerably more robust than the same reply to an opening bid. If the bidding has proceeded 1♣-1♠-No and you are fourth to speak with:

$$♠64 \quad ♡AJ7 \quad ◇KQ83 \quad ♣QJ95$$

a bid of 3NT is simply punishing partner for his enterprise. He has made what may be a very weak overcall, bearing in mind its high pre-emptive value. Even facing a vulnerable overcall, this hand is worth no more than 2NT; and if the bid was not vulnerable, the only safe course is to start with a U.C.B. of 2♣, intending to pass if partner can do no more than repeat his spades.

OPENER'S SECOND BID

By the time the bidding comes back to the opener it may have developed in a wide variety of ways. We may still be at the 1-level, or wondering whether to introduce a second suit at the level of five. In the remaining pages of this chapter we shall examine some of the more common sequences and consider how opener should handle them.

(i) 1♣-1♠-No-No

Responder's pass here is virtually forcing! Only if he has opened on a flat minimum or if he suspects a bad misfit should the opener consider passing (against competent opponents, at least). Responder may have as much as 7-8 points, and neither opponent seems to think much of his hand. With most sound opening bids, the best solution is to re-open with a double, which will be examined in detail later on. A minimum rebid in opener's original suit, or a second suit, is simply a competitive move on a moderate distributional hand.

Apart from the re-opening double, stronger bids available to the opener here are 1NT, a jump in a new suit (or a reverse), and a bid of opponents' suit. A jump rebid of the original suit is rarely wise – right-hand opponent is quite likely to hold this suit, and strong one-suiters can be developed more safely by starting with a double.

The re-opening 1NT should show about 16-19 points with a solid guard in the enemy suit. It is possible to agree to play the bid as showing a wider range, in which case responder needs a Crowhurst-style 2♣ inquiry.

A jump in a new suit, or a reverse, cannot logically be forcing – opener could not start with a forcing bid, and responder may have passed for the sufficient reason that he holds a Yarborough! Such bids show two-suited hands of considerable playing strength:

$$♠7 \quad ♡AQ865 \quad ◇9 \quad ♣AKJ843$$

Playing standard Acol you have little alternative to an opening 1♣ on this hand. If the bidding then proceeds 1◇-No-No you have the right cards for a non-forcing 2♡; if the overcall was 1♠ instead of 1◇ a reverse of 2♡ would still be enough. The message is that you expect to take a lot of tricks but cannot re-open with a double as you would not welcome a penalty pass from your partner. With a less shapely hand such as this:

$$♠7 \quad ♡AQJ6 \quad ◇KQ9 \quad ♣AK653$$

it would be quite wrong to bid 2♡ after 1♣-1♠-No-No. This hand is ideally suited for a re-opening double – if partner passes for penalties, holding 5 good spades and nothing else, the defence should be enjoyable.

A re-opening cue-bid is understandably a rare event. Having opened with a one-bid opener suddenly discovers an extra ace and asks his partner to pick a suit at the 3-level. The bid describes a maximum three-suited opening bid and virtually guarantees a void in opponents' suit. Something like this:

♠KQ64   ♡–   ◇AK97   ♣KQJ86

You open 1♣ with this hand, and a 1♡ overcall on your left is followed by two passes. A 2♡ bid now describes your hand well, and partner should be able to make an informed decision. When this hand was dealt, responder in fact held:

♠J53   ♡862   ◇Q8542   ♣A9

He jumped straight to 5◇, and was roundly castigated by his partner for not bidding the cold slam! His defence was that no one could reasonably envisage a slam after an opening one-bid and a pass by responder, an argument which failed to impress his audience. Once opener is known to be void you can rely on something like 25 points in a 30-point pack – what more do you want?

Note that a re-opening double on such hands would be too dangerous. If responder has quite rightly passed the 1♡ overcall with:

♠753   ♡KJ1094   ◇Q3   ♣752

he will now leave the double in, and instead of playing in a reasonable 3NT you will be struggling to collect a small penalty. Over the re-opening cue-bid, a jump to 3NT would be in order with this hand.

(ii) 1♣-1NT-No-No
This is a good time to go quietly, and the more you have in high cards the more quietly you should go. A double would be for penalties, confirming that you would like partner to lead your suit, but this is rarely a sensible move – with his rubbishy hand he is going to lead your suit anyway, and the double simply gives opponents a chance to reconsider and seek a safer haven. To rebid your original suit would be another way of asking for

trouble. The most likely type of hand to justify re-opening is a strong two-suiter, and even here a quiet minimum bid in the second suit is enough:

♠AQJ32 ♡95 ◇AK1086 ♣A

You open 1♠ on this hand with high hopes, but after 1NT on your left and two passes the prospects are bleak. With the spades stacked on your left and a worthless hand opposite you are not going to make many tricks, and a restrained bid of 2◇ now is quite courageous enough.

(iii) 1♣-2◇-No-No
A strong jump overcall affords no great cause for alarm. Your right-hand opponent must be fairly bad to pass it, and your partner may well hold some useful values, especially if you are not playing Sputnik doubles in these sequences. No conventional subtleties are needed here – if you have a sensible bid you make it, and if not you pass.

(iv) 1♣-3◇-No-No
When the hand on your left has pre-empted you should rarely re-open. Your partner should have taken any reasonable risk to find a bid, and if he has passed it is a safe bet that your right-hand opponent is silently imploring you to stick your neck out. Disappoint him. Only a very powerful distributional hand justifies re-opening in this exposed position; with anything less, pass, and if it turns out badly blame your partner.

(v) 1♣-1♠-2◇-No
If your partner bids freely after the overcall, no problem arises when he raises your suit or calls no trumps. You will be a little less confident than usual that a raise is based on 4-card support, and you may occasionally be anxious about your joint holding in the enemy suit when he bids no trumps, but these are minor points. It is when partner introduces a new suit that the situation can become awkward. Consider this one:

♠Q9 ♡AKJ4 ◇J5 ♣Q9864

You open 1♣, next hand overcalls 1♠, your partner bids 2♦ and fourth hand passes. In standard methods the 2♦ response is forcing, and you clearly have no possible bid but 2♡, which is all very well so long as partner does not expect you to have reversing values. He shouldn't expect it, but many will.

Again, you might hold something of this sort:

♠KJ95   ♡K76   ♦83   ♣AJ92

The bidding begins in the same fashion, 1♣-1♠-2♦-No, and clearly any rebid from you other than 2NT is inconceivable, but are you sure your partner is not going to read that as the usual 15-16 and raise you to game on a scruffy 10-count?

Unless you are playing Sputnik doubles, and the associated non-forcing free bids, of which much more later, it is essential to accept that the opener in such sequences must be allowed to make strong-sounding rebids on minimum hands. On the first hand shown above he must be able to rebid a non-forcing 2♡; on the second, 2NT. Such solutions are far from ideal: on the second hand, for instance, even 2NT may be too high, or partner with an attractive 11-count may be unsure whether to make the push to game. But as long as the change-of-suit response is forcing (and it must be, so long as Sputnik is not being used) you have to bid something.

We may summarize the position as follows. If the intervention has forced responder to bid his suit at a higher level than the opener would have envisaged, then a 'reverse' by opener is non-forcing and promises no extra values; and a minimum no-trump rebid shows a minimum hand. This rule allows a distinction to be made between apparently similar sequences.

(a) 1♣-1♠-2♡-No   (b) 1♦-1♠-2♣-No
    2NT   2NT

In the case of sequence (a), opener would have allowed for a 1♡ response, but not for 2♡, and 2NT is therefore weak. In (b) opener could have anticipated a 2♣ response even without the intervention, and 2NT should now be full value.

(c) 1♣-1♠-2♦-No   (d) 1♣-1♦-1♠-No
    2♡   2♡

In (c) the opener is saying no more than that he would have

rebid 1♡ over a 1◇ response, but in (d) the overcall has not affected the level of the response, and the opener is showing reversing values.

There remains the question of what the opener should do when he has a stronger hand but has been robbed of his appropriate rebid:

♠AQ6 ♡94 ◇KJ8 ♣AQ832

After 1♣-1♠-2♡-No, this hand is too good for the weak 2NT, and should bid 3NT direct, trusting partner to have at least a useful 9-count for his embarrassing response.

♠7 ♡AQJ8 ◇K93 ♣AK1064

Here, after 1♣-1♠-2◇-No, you want to make a forcing reverse of 2♡, but this is not available. A jump to 3♡ is possible but cumbersome. The best solution is to bid 2♠, the enemy suit, and show the hearts next time if appropriate – this type of cue-bid should be played as forcing to suit-agreement, whereas an immediate 3♡ would be forcing to game.

Reverting for a moment to the situation where partner has raised your opening bid, a point which rarely seems to be discussed in books on bidding is the meaning of a 'trial bid' in the enemy suit. For instance, if the bidding has begun 1♠-2◇-2♠-No, what would 3◇ mean? In the absence of specific agreement one would perhaps take it as a short-suit trial bid, but this is probably not the most efficient use, as your partner will be unsurprised to learn you are short in the enemy suit. It makes more sense to reserve the bid for a hand of this sort:

♠KQJ5 ♡AQ7 ◇Q92 ♣AJ6

where you would like to play 3NT if partner has only three spades and a bolster in diamonds. If your own side has been bidding a minor, of course, 3NT may still be best even if partner does hold 4-card support

(vi) 1♣-1♠-2◇-2♠
The problems arising when all four players have bid will be discussed in Chapter 8, dealing with competitive doubles.

(vii) 1◇-No-1♡-2♣

This type of sequence is similar to the one examined under (v) above, and is likely to cause similar mishaps. For instance:

$$\spadesuit AQ65 \quad \heartsuit 97 \quad \diamondsuit AKJ86 \quad \clubsuit 63$$

You open 1◇, next hand passes, partner replies 1♡, and right-hand opponent comes in with 2♣. The natural bid may appear to be 2◇, but this is tactically bad – if next hand raises the clubs there is considerable risk that you will miss a productive 4-4 spade fit. Again, after the same bidding you may hold:

$$\spadesuit KQ9 \quad \heartsuit QJ7 \quad \diamondsuit AKQ3 \quad \clubsuit J64$$

where there seems no convenient bid available except 3♣, which may push you over the top if partner has scratched up a minimum response on a 5-count.

The essential point about such auctions is that it is quite impossible that the overcall should become the final contract. You have opened, partner has changed the suit, so how can it be right to let your opponents play undoubled at the level of one or two? Once this principle is accepted, the solution is easy: *a pass by the opener is forcing*! This simple arrangement completely solves opener's problems – if his natural rebid is still available he makes it, and if not he passes. Of the two extra bids placed at his disposal by the overcall, a double is normally for penalties (though we shall suggest later a better alternative use), and a cue-bid of opponents' suit is strong, and suggests in the first instance an interest in no trumps.

As for the responder to the forcing pass, he is free to make any bid that further describes his hand, and when he has no natural bid available he can always resort to a double, which is merely co-operative in this position – a pure penalty double at this level by the player sitting under the overcall is unlikely to be very profitable.

Further suggestions for improving the accuracy of the opening side's exchanges in such sequences will be found at the end of Chapter 7, in the section entitled 'Opener's Sputnik'.

(viii) 1♣-No-No-1♠

This sequence is only superficially similar to the one described under (i) above. The opener is now taking a considerable risk if he bids again. Partner is known to be pathetically weak, right-hand opponent can do no more than muster a protective over-call (for the implications of this, see Chapter 6), so most of the missing high cards are sitting on your left, and the only reason that your left-hand opponent has passed must be that he is stacked in your suit. When in any doubt, pass, not least because your partner is still there, and will no doubt scrape up some sort of bid if (improbably) the overcall runs round to him.

OVERCALLER'S SECOND BID

In most cases the overcaller's second turn will present few problems. A natural bid or, more likely, a pass will usually suggest itself. However, there is one interesting area to be examined: the meaning of a double by a player who could manage nothing more impressive than a simple overcall on the previous round. There are several distinct cases to consider.

(i) 1♣-1♠-No-No
      2♣-Dbl

It is not impossible for the overcaller to want to double for penalties in this sequence, but it is unlikely. A more economical use is to play this type of double as showing a maximum overcall in terms of high cards but with a moderate suit and some support for the unbid suits. The overcaller may hold:

♠KJ965   ♡A84   ◇KQ63   ♣5

Having reasonably decided to show the spades first rather than doubling, he can now complete a good picture of his hand with a second-round double. This is a much more helpful effort than 2◇, which would suggest a two-suited hand with poor hearts.

If the 2♣ bid had come from responder, the double would have a similar meaning though without such a firm inference of high-card strength, as the double would now be made in the protective position.

(ii) 1♣-1♡-No-No
       1♠-Dbl

When the opener has bid two suits, the double is more penalty-oriented. The doubler in this sequence may well hold both majors and be scenting a misfit. If he has a red two-suiter, he can simply bid 2 ◇, so a double is not needed in any take-out sense.

(iii)   1◇-1♠-2♣-No
2◇-Dbl

This is an unlikely adventure by the doubler, with his left-hand opponent still unlimited and an obvious bid available to show the fourth suit. The most likely explanation is that he holds a hand of this type:

♠AK876   ♡K5   ◇K984   ♣52

where he has hopes of a penalty if his partner holds the clubs and expects to come to no harm in 2♠ if that is all his partner can bid.

   If the first overcall in that sequence had been 1♡, however, a double would be very useful to show a hand of this type:

♠KQ93   ♡AQ876   ◇K92   ♣2

Not liking to double 1◇ with a singleton club, you elect to overcall 1♡, but the 2♣ response may make it impossible for partner to show spades, and a spade fit may now be lost. Regular partnerships may find it helpful to agree that when the fourth suit cannot be shown at a safe level a double shows this suit. The same principle could be extended to our sequence (ii), where if the first overcall was 1◇ the overcaller cannot now show a secondary heart suit.

(iv)   1♡-1♠-No-2◇
2♡-Dbl

This type of double is clearly for penalties. Partner has shown some values but with no liking for spades, and if we have a good overcall with something in hearts and poor diamonds an early double should pay off. The doubler might have:

♠AQ873   ♡K106   ◇5   ♣KJ83

On the evidence so far, this is a good time to defend.

   When partner has bid but one or both sides have found a fit, the double comes into the 'competitive' category, and will be discussed in a later chapter.

3. The take-out double

The ide᾿ of the take-out or informatory double is older than Contract Bridge itself, dating from the early days of Auction. In the sophisticated modern language of bidding the double has acquired a number of unnatural or conventional meanings, but the original take-out double of the opening suit bid of one has staunchly resisted the wind of change. The message conveyed by this type of double is 'I should like to compete in the auction but am not prepared to suggest a trump suit at this stage' – contrast this with the message of the suit overcall, 'I should like to compete in this suit and probably no other.'

The take-out double is used in many other situations, and this leads to frequent problems of recognition. How is one to be sure whether partner's double is a request for one to bid, or whether he is licking his lips in expectation of a huge penalty? A careful study of his facial expression provides an easy if unethical solution; fortunately there exists an almost equally simple rule of thumb which, with a few exceptions, defines standard modern practice:

Any double of a suit bid at the 1- or 2-level is for take-out provided that (a) the doubler's partner has not bid, (b) it is not a double of a rebid unsupported suit, and (c) opponents have not bid more than two suits.

In this chapter we shall examine some of the commonest types of take-out double, and also identify the most frequent cases where what sounds like a take-out double is in fact for penalties, and vice versa.

A. DOUBLING THE OPENING ONE OF A SUIT

This double, which is always for take-out, is used on hands which are unsuitable for a simple overcall, either because they contain no single good suit, or because they are too strong. As contrasted with the overcall, the double has its drawbacks. Its tactical value is nil, since it actually increases the bidding-space available to opponents, who now have the extra choice of redoubling or passing to see which way the wind blows. The bid also has an enormous range, being made on anything from a weak three-suiter to an Acol Two bid. Despite this, the doubler's partner may often be able to judge at once that his hand is going to be very useful. With this hand:

♠KJ976   ♡4   ◇Q10876   ♣K6

you would face a tricky problem in valuation after 1♡ on your left, 2♣ from partner, No Bid on your right; but if instead your partner has doubled 1♡ you can be sure there are game chances – either partner will have a good fit for your spades or he will have enough strength to offer a play for game in some other denomination.

Most authorities in discussing this type of double stress the need for a high degree of preparedness. The ideal hand for a double of 1♡ is a 4-1-4-4 shape, preferably with a couple of honours in each unbid suit and with at least the values for a non-minimum opening bid. Any distributional shortcomings, they say, must be compensated for by extra high-card strength. The modern outlook is less dogmatic, though naturally you must use your judgement if you wish to relax the distributional requirements: remember the message of the double, and be sure that it is the message you want to convey. World Championship bridge is full of doubles which would have outraged the pundits of yesteryear – for instance, Mike Lawrence of the U.S. Aces doubled an opening 1◇ on:

♠AQ3   ♡1086   ◇K106   ♣AJ82

Without suggesting you should go as far as that, we simply make the point that many players put too tight a restriction on the requirements for a double, and thus obtain less value than they should from this highly flexible weapon. All the following hands justify a take-out double of 1 ♡ in the modern game:

(a) ♠KJ84   (b) ♠Q765   (c) ♠KQ3
    ♡73   ♡9   ♡2
    ◇AQ6   ◇A10854   ◇KQ98
    ♣K954   ♣AQ3   ♣AJ853

Hand (a) is about as weak as you should ever be for the bid. Make the fourth spade into a fourth diamond and it would be sounder to pass. Hand (b) is much better described by a double than by a bid in the sketchy diamond suit – if partner is so inconsiderate as to bid clubs you will simply have to pass. Hand (c), the best of the three, is paradoxically the least satisfactory double as it contains only three spades; however, it is essentially a three-suited hand, and the extra high-card strength makes up for the lack of preparedness for the all-important spade suit.

So we may define the requirements for the modern-style take-out double as follows: the bid shows opening values and *if minimum* must contain at least three cards in any unbid suit, with preferably at least four in any unbid major. The emphasis on majors is crucial: one might bend the rule to admit a double on a 5-4-2-2 shape when both suits are majors, knowing that partner will strain to respond in a major if he possibly can . . . but if you do decide to double an opening 1 ◇ on:

♠KJ76 ♡AQJ84 ◇92 ♣Q6

and partner replies 2♣ you will just have to stand your ground. A change of suit by the doubler on the second round promises considerably better values than this.

That, in fact, is the yardstick for dealing with hands which are too strong for a suit overcall yet are principally one-suited. The minimum range for a take-out double followed by a change of suit is about 15 high-card points and at least 5 cards in the suit you intend to introduce. If the suit contains 6 or more cards you will only need to double when you have a hand in the Acol Two range, too good for a strong jump overcall, and in this case you make a *jump* rebid in your suit.

Two-suited hands should rarely be introduced with a double.

Unless the hand is simply too strong to risk it, the best method is to make a normal overcall in one suit intending to bid the other next time. With this hand:

♠KJ954 ♡AQ1032 ◇K2 ♣6

after an opening 1♣ on your left the best bid is 1♠, for you can bid hearts next time if the signs are right. A double would be quite unsound: after a not unlikely 2◇ response you would have to bid one of your majors, forcing after the jump response, and you will now have difficulty stopping out of game on what may well be a combined 21-count and a misfit. If you dislike the idea of a non-forcing 1♠ overcall on the hand shown, you have our sympathy . . . and you also have an easy remedy available in the Michaels Cuebid, an excellent competitive gadget which we shall be examining in Chapter 5.

The final type of hand which has to be launched with a take-out double is one on which you would like to bid no trumps but which is too strong for an immediate 1NT overcall; with these hands double first and bid no trumps later – how many no trumps is a point we shall consider when we come to deal with the doubler's rebid.

To conclude this section, here are some examples of stronger types of hand which are suitable for a take-out double of (in this case) 1◇:

(a) ♠AKJ65   (b) ♠A7   (c) ♠KJ4
    ♡82   ♡AKQ1054   ♡A53
    ◇K4   ◇AQ6   ◇KQ10
    ♣AK63   ♣32   ♣AQ75

Hand (a) is weak in hearts but is far too strong for a 1♠ overcall at any vulnerability, so you must double first and then bid the spades. With hand (b) you would have opened an Acol 2♡, so start with a double intending to make a forcing jump bid in hearts next time. Hand (c) is too good for any normal-range 1NT overcall, and again you should double first, intending to bid no trumps later.

B. DOUBLES WHEN BOTH OPPONENTS HAVE BID

Modern experts are keen to compete with moderate values and fair distribution. Whenever they are unable to select one of the unbid suits, out comes the take-out double. Compare these two hands after the bidding 1♣-No-1♡:

(a) ♠KQ1097   (b) ♠K10974
     ♡4   ♡4
     ◇J742   ◇AQ104
     ♣AQ3   ♣K103

On hand (a) a 1♠ overcall is better, emphasizing the good suit, but on hand (b) a double is infinitely superior, offering partner a choice of contracts (or of opening leads, if you end up defending).

With this hand:

♠AJ94 ♡Q853 ◇A64 ♣K4

boldness by Bob Goldman of the U.S. Aces steered his side into a makable game on minimum values after the auction had started 1◇-No-2♣. Goldman doubled and found his partner, Mike Lawrence, with:

♠1062 ♡AJ106 ◇K8532 ♣2

After the next hand had raised to 3♣, Lawrence went straight to 4♡, which became the final contract. There were no problems in the play, and the U.S.A. scored +420.

One may be even more daring when the opponents have bid and supported a suit. Once they have established a fit, you are mathematically more likely to find partner at home in one of the unbid suits. Here are two examples of take-out doubles in this situation:

(a) ♠73   (b) ♠KJ62
     ♡5   ♡74
     ◇KJ1084   ◇A983
     ♣KQ1093   ♣K86

On hand (a) after 1♡-No-1♠-No-2♠ it may seem risky to force partner to bid at the 3-level when you have a mere 9 points, but the risk of a penalty is less than the possible gain if you find a satisfactory fit. The Unusual No Trump, if used, would of course handle this position equally well. On hand (b) you are just too weak to risk a take-out double of an opening 1♡ on your right, but if this is raised to 2♡ on your left and passed back to you, you have the ideal hand to re-open with a double.

Hand (a) in fact comes from a recent team-of-four match, and the player who refused to enter the bidding on these cards lost substantially when his opposite number in the other room displayed more courage. After the bidding described, the latter player came in with a double, and when his side eventually sacrificed in 5♣ over the opposing 4♡ their opponents misjudged, as often happens, and doubled for an inadequate penalty of 300, with eleven tricks cold in either major the other way.

C. TAKE-OUT DOUBLES AT HIGHER LEVELS

At higher levels, the double assumes a slightly different character. A low-level double is normally passed for penalties only when the responder's trump holding is so powerful that it appears likely that his opponents are intending to play in his own side's best suit. At the 3-level or higher, a double retains its take-out meaning if the circumstances comply with the requirements outlined above, yet it may be passed more freely on a fair defensive hand. After the sequence 1♡-No-3♡, therefore, it is safe to double with:

♠KQ106 ♡8 ◇AK853 ♣KJ3

but not with:

♠A6432 ♡KQ109 ◇7 ♣852

or:

♠AK ♡54 ◇KQJ1074 ♣AQ8

In the example sequence (1♡-No-3♡-Dbl), the doubler's partner could pass with:

♠75 ♡A73 ◇7642 ♣A874

or:

♠953 ♡QJ10 942 ♣A874

This type of high-level double is sometimes called 'optional'.

D. THE MODERN USE OF THE DOUBLE

The examples quoted in the previous section show that the modern expert uses the take-out double not merely to instigate a constructive sequence but also to ensure that his side can compete vigorously when the balance of strength is more or less evenly divided. Even when the opening side has virtually guaranteed the bigger share of the high cards, as with an Acol Two opening or a jump response to a suit opening, a take-out double may enable opponents to sacrifice, to interfere pre-emptively, or even to find a makable game on tenuous high-card values. For example:

North-South Game, Dealer South

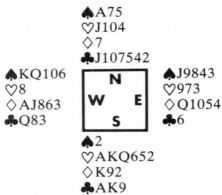

```
              ♠A75
              ♡J104
              ◇7
              ♣J107542
♠KQ106                      ♠J9843
♡8          N               ♡973
◇AJ863    W   E             ◇Q1054
♣Q83          S             ♣6
              ♠2
              ♡AKQ652
              ◇K92
              ♣AK9
```

South opened with an Acol 2♡, and with East-West silent throughout North-South bid 2♡-2NT-3♡-4♡, making eleven tricks for +650. A Gold Cup match might have had a different result if West had doubled the opening bid:

South	West	North	East
2♡	Dbl	3♡	3♠
4♡	No	No	4♠
No	No	Dbl	No
No	No		

And unless South switches to a diamond before East gains the lead, East-West will score a double game swing. Even after an accurate defence, the minimal penalty will be a fair reward for buccaneering tactics in this field of bidding.

When the take-out double is used against the weight of the cards, the distribution should be good, and the hand must infallibly contain support for all the unbid suits. Moderate balanced hands which would qualify for a 'modern' double of a one-bid should be passed after an opening two-bid, or any similar bid making it clear that opponents have the balance of strength.

Try this example. You hold at Love All:

♠AJ107   ♡8   ◇KJ1053   ♣743

The bidding against you begins with 1♣ on your left and 2♡ on your right. Would you compete?

Perhaps you would not have thought of a take-out double, but the expert who held the hand in a high-stake rubber game did, and the full deal turned out to be:

Love All, Dealer South

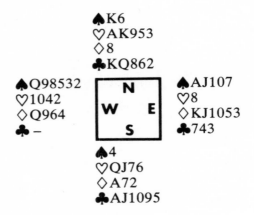

```
                      ♠K6
                      ♡AK953
                      ◇8
                      ♣KQ862
        ♠Q98532    ┌─────────┐   ♠AJ107
        ♡1042      │    N    │   ♡8
        ◇Q964      │ W     E │   ◇KJ1053
        ♣ –        │    S    │   ♣743
                   └─────────┘
                      ♠4
                      ♡QJ76
                      ◇A72
                      ♣AJ1095
```

The auction proceeded:

South	West	North	East
1♣	No	2♡	Dbl
3♡	6♠(!)	Dbl	No
No	No		

This contract was defeated by two tricks when North led his ♡A and switched to his singleton diamond. Although North-South can be defeated double-dummy in 6♡ by a club ruff, the East-West players were well satisfied with their 300-point 'insurance' – the more so since no defence defeats 6♣.

E. DOUBLES BY THE OPENING SIDE

Informatory doubles also occur in this common situation, but they merge in theory with the 'competitive' double, described later. However, the simplest case can be examined here – the double by opener of an immediate or protective overcall when partner has passed. This situation conforms in all respects to the requirements for a take-out double and is accordingly identical in meaning. An example would be:

South	West	North	East
1♡	2♣	No	No
Dbl			

It is true that South might be faced with a dilemma in this position if he held:

♠64 ♡AKJ85 ◇A5 ♣KQ109

As in other similar cases he must ruefully pass and settle for the probable small plus score. This will surely represent the best possible result for his side on the hand. The advantage that would accrue from being able to make a penalty double after this sequence is easily outweighed by two considerations. First, it would be an untimely warning to opponents, who may well have a better spot available in diamonds or spades; secondly, the opener would be forced to make an unsatisfactory bid with either of these more frequent hands:

(a) ♠AJ86   (b) ♠AQ5
     ♡KQJ8   ♡AQ752
     ◇AJ52   ◇A854
     ♣6   ♣6

In both cases a bid of 2◇ would suggest a more two-suited type of hand. A double is more flexible, and also caters for a responder who was too weak to make a penalty double of 2♣, but is content to pass the re-opening double, perhaps with a hand such as:

♠K74   ♡43   ♢963   ♣Q10743

Finally, it should be noted that if Sputnik doubles are being used the opener will need to re-open with a double on a wider range of hands than we have so far examined. We shall return to this question in Chapter 7.

F. SOME SPECIAL CASES

When both opponents are in the bidding, the double can assume interesting and sometimes confusing shades of meaning. In this section we shall look at a few cases in which the doubler's partner may not be quite sure what the double is telling him.

(i) 1NT-No-2♡-Dbl

It is a well established principle that all doubles of no-trump bids are for penalties, but suppose that as here opponents run from no trumps before you get a chance to double them – what is the double now? (We are assuming that the 2♡ bid is a natural 'weak take-out').

Standard practice is to treat the double in such cases as being for take-out. Some players prefer to give it a slightly different meaning, so that the double says in effect, 'I would have doubled 1NT had the responder not rescued.' However, it is recognized that this type of double cannot be passed without an adequate trump holding; therefore it cannot logically be made without some preparedness for all the unbid suits. Consider this hand:

♠KQ107   ♡AK643   ♢8   ♣A84

After the bidding 1NT-No-2♡, do you take any action? A double is permissible according to the second interpretation suggested above, but is all too likely to lead to exchanging a small profit from 2♡ undoubled for a loss in some diamond contract. We consider it better to treat the double as a normal take-out one, and pass hands such as this one. Our advice is: double with shortage in the bid suit and opening values, or with any powerful balanced hand.

(ii) 1♠-No-1NT-Dbl
This is an exception to the rule that all doubles of no-trump bids are for penalties. The doubler here has a sound take-out double of 1♠. He should be able to stand a penalty pass if his partner has the spades well held, but in principle he is expecting to hear a bid.

(iii) 1♣-1♠-2◇-Dbl
Our rule-of-thumb classes this as a penalty double, since partner has bid . . . but why double a forcing 2◇ for penalties when for all you know it is about to be raised to 3◇? The important point here is to be sure that the 2◇ bid *is* forcing – it is in standard methods, but not if the bidder is playing Sputnik (or has previously passed). If the bid is forcing, the only sensible use for the double is to play it as 'competitive' (see Chapter 8); if not, double for penalties.

**(iv) 1♣-No-1♠-No
    2♣-Dbl**
This is a double of a rebid unsupported suit, and is therefore for penalties. The assumption is that the doubler has been forced to make a trap pass over 1♣, on some such holding as:

♠85 ♡K76 ◇AK9 ♣AQ1042

Now that the clubs have been rebid, the trapper can emerge from hiding with excellent prospects of collecting a satisfactory penalty.

Note that there is no need to double in this position on a weak red two-suiter, such as:

♠64 ♡AQ98 ◇KJ532 ♣87

The responder is as yet unlimited, and if he passes this time your partner will surely protect if he sees fair chances of competing in one of the unbid suits. It is worth remarking that if you are desperate to compete on this hand, having passed throughout on every hand for the last hour, you can always introduce 2◇ – after your initial pass you would not take this risk unless you had hearts as a second string.

(v) 1♣-No-1NT-No
2♣-Dbl

This sequence may look very similar to (iv), but there are some important differences. Here, both opponents are limited; moreover, the opener can be almost sure of finding an adequate club fit in dummy. You are unlikely to hold a promising trap-pass hand here, and the double can be more sensibly used to show a weak hand with good distribution, such as:

♠J864 ♡KQ76 ◇A8532 ♣ –

When the opening bid was in a major suit, however, rather different considerations apply. Now there is no reason whatever to expect opener's partner to have any fit at all, though the opener himself is sure of holding a 6-card suit. In the modern game, a 1NT response to one of a major may be made on a distributional hand of about 5-8 points with no tolerance for opener's suit. Although we agree with the desirability of leaving plenty of scope for vigorous competition at the part-score level, it seems silly to dispense with the gelignite when opponents tread on our booby-trap. The following type of situation occurs with sufficient frequency to justify retaining the double of a major in such positions in its old sense:

Dealer North, Game All

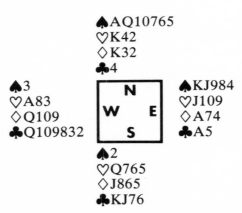

North opens 1♠, and clearly East can do nothing but pass for the moment. South replies 1NT in the hope of improving the contract, but North reasonably rebids his spades. With both opponents limited and the trumps spectacularly stacked in his favour, East is well placed for a punishing double of 2♠; he leads the Jack of Hearts, and even if North manages to save a trick by end-playing East, the defence can still come to one club, two diamonds, two hearts and three trumps for a useful 800 penalty.

(vi) 1♣-Dbl-1♠-No
2♣-Dbl

Another, more obvious exception to the 'rebid unsupported suit' rule: you will rarely hold a take-out double of 1♣ on the first round and a sound penalty double of 2♣ on the second, so you are simply showing a good take-out double and again asking partner to bid. As a matter of interest, you should by no means rule out the possibility of playing in spades – the 1♠ bid could well be psychic, as the position is a favourite one for joke bids of all kinds.

(vii) 1♣-No-1♠-No
2♣-No-No-Dbl

A final, tricky variation on the 'rebid unsupported suit' theme. West will bid on virtually any thirteen cards in his position, and could have passed on the first round with a variety of strongish hands. It seems illogical to give this double its 'standard' meaning of a trap pass based on good clubs – sitting under the club bidder you are not well placed for this sort of action, and your double is likely to make the play easier. Our preference here is to treat the double as 'co-operative', with good *spades* rather than clubs, and at least tolerance for both unbid suits. With this hand:

$$♠KQ107 \quad ♡AJ43 \quad ◇KQ9 \quad ♣62$$

you would refrain from entering the bidding on the first round, hoping opponents are heading for a nasty accident in spades; when they subside in 2♣ you can enter the fray with a double, hoping partner will have enough clubs to pass (as is likely) but fully prepared for a retreat into one of the red suits.

**(viii) 1♣-No-1♡-No
       1NT-No-No-Dbl**

This is a similar situation to the last one. The double is for penalties, and partner should lead a heart. It would be folly to double here on any old balanced 16-count – you should have a strong heart suit. Note that as in many similar cases there are other ways of competing if you want partner to bid – in the present case a bid of 2♣ would clearly offer a choice between diamonds and spades.

**(ix) 1♠-No-1NT-No
       No-Dbl**

Apparently similar to (ii), this is really more like (vii) or (viii). The doubler expects to defeat 1NT . . . providing he gets a spade lead.

**(x) 1♣-1♡-No-1♠
      Dbl**

We conclude this section by looking at a few doubles by the opening side. This one is an unusual type, and would no doubt cause some head-scratching at the table. The most practical explanation is that the doubler has a hand of this type:

♠K9 ♡64 ◇AQ53 ♣KQJ75

He is unwilling to surrender just yet, and neither 2♣ nor 2◇ is entirely satisfactory. By playing a double in this position to show the unbid suit you can tell partner about the diamond holding without venturing beyond the level of 2♣. This type of double may be regarded as a take-out double offering a choice between two suits, yet catering for the very occasional penalty conversion.

With this hand:

♠AQJ6 ♡87 ◇K10 ♣AK973

you may wish that after the bidding given you could make a penalty or lead-directing double of 1♠, but this fish should not get off the hook in any case. If your partner has:

♠53 ♡QJ54 ◇Q7642 ♣Q8

and the 1♠ bid runs round to him it is not too difficult for him to place you with a strong hand, and he should re-open with a double. A double by the responder in this position is theoretically for penalties, but it is difficult to imagine what kind of hand he could have to justify this action, and a more sensible treatment is to play the double as 'competitive', based on the type of hand shown above. Now a penalty pass from you should produce a good result. This introduces a point which will occur again: a penalty pass is if anything a more effective weapon than a penalty double, since only one opponent has a chance to bid after hearing the bad news.

(xi) 1♣-Dbl-No-1♡
      Dbl

Clearly for take-out. This may seem a rather rash enterprise by the opener, but he must allow for the possibility of a minimum double. He may hold:

♠KQ7 ♡10 ◇AK64 ♣AJ852

This type of double should be used sparingly, on good hands with no sensible alternative bid available. With a fourth spade instead of a fourth diamond, for instance, it would be more practical to bid 1♠ after the bidding given.

(xii) 1♣-No-No-Dbl
       No-1♠-Dbl

This sequence led to disaster in a club duplicate pairs when the opener assumed the double to be for penalties and passed it. Although a double when partner has bid *is* normally for penalties, a little thought shows that interpretation to be absurd here. The doubler could not reply to a 1♣ opening, and the opener has shown nothing extra, so how can the doubler reasonably expect to defeat 1♠? He in fact held:

♠7 ♡Q1098 ◇J9643 ♣852

and his imaginative effort deserved a better fate. His partner had:

♠A63 ♡6 ◇A1085 ♣AK976

and if he had interpreted the double correctly would have been able to compete up to the 4-level in either minor for a good score.

(xiii) 1NT-No-2♣-2♡
Dbl

A common situation – the 2♣ bid is Stayman, we assume. It is normal to play the double as essentially for penalties, showing 4 cards in the overcaller's suit. An extension which has been found useful occurs when the overcall is in spades and the opener holds 4 hearts – it would be possible here to play a double as Sputnik-type, showing the unbid major, but this could result in a missed penalty and in any case puts some strain on the memory. A better arrangement is for the opener to bid 2NT with 4 hearts and a minimum 1NT, 3 of his better minor with 4 hearts and a maximum. This may run into trouble if the Stayman bidder is very weak, but that is a lesser risk than missing a good heart game, as you may well do if you pass.

(xiv) 1NT-No-2♡-2♠
Dbl

Although no existing treatise on doubles in competition has discussed the meaning of a double in this very common position, common sense suggests that here is another very obvious exception to the rule that doubles when partner has bid are for penalties. If 2♡ is natural and possibly very weak, the opener cannot reasonably expect to enjoy defending 2♠. This double can therefore be freed for use as a 'competitive' type, saying in effect, 'I have a very good fit for your hearts, and if you are maximum they may be sorry they bid.' The opener may have:

♠764 ♡AQ97 ◇AJ104 ♣K6

and a competitive-type double from him will produce a delight-ful result if his partner holds:

♠9 ♡J106532 ◇Q84 ♣A53

Finally, a deal from rubber bridge which horrifically illus-trates what is perhaps the most important point about doubles in competition – if your partner makes a double in an unusual or confused situation, a little thought will usually enable you to disinter his meaning, where blanket adherence to rules of thumb can lead to castatrophe.

Love All, Dealer East

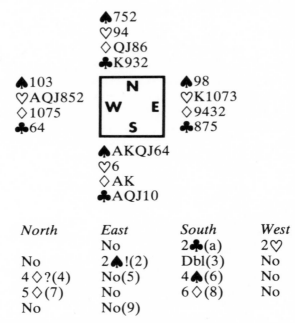

```
                    ♠752
                    ♡94
                    ◇QJ86
                    ♣K932
        ♠103          N          ♠98
        ♡AQJ852                   ♡K1073
        ◇1075    W       E        ◇9432
        ♣64           S           ♣875
                    ♠AKQJ64
                    ♡6
                    ◇AK
                    ♣AQJ10
```

North	East	South	West
	No	2♣(a)	2♡
No	2♠!(2)	Dbl(3)	No
4◇?(4)	No(5)	4♠(6)	No
5◇(7)	No	6◇(8)	No
No	No(9)		

1) Normal Acol – the blockbuster bid.

2) Worth a try at rubber bridge. Opponents may get their wires crossed.

3) Obviously for penalties. If East is genuine, North-South are well out of it; if not, a penalty of 1500 will more than compensate for a missed slam.

4) A dreadful bid. North simply applies the normal doubling rules – he himself has not bid, spades are not a rebid unsupported suit, opponents have bid only two suits, therefore the double is for take-out. But if South wants his partner to bid here, he has only to pass! A minor point is that if North really is incapable of understanding the double, 4◇ is still absurdly unilateral – he should bid 3♡, showing useful values and allowing his partner to pick the suit.

5) Content to sit back and watch.

6) Cautious but reasonable – South tries to suggest that his spades are good enough even if East really has them.

7) North decides that South has made a cue-bid in support of diamonds, and signs off in the agreed suit.

8) South now places his partner with something like:

♠2 ♡K85 ◇QJ10876 ♣654

in which case 6◇ should be easy.

9) Perhaps he should bid 6♡, but if South goes 6♠ over this even North can hardly misinterpret it! It seems better to leave well alone and hope that 6◇ can be beaten. In fact the only defence to beat 6◇ is to start with two rounds of hearts, promoting a trump trick for East's ◇9, and this was duly done, completing a good afternoon's work for the defenders.

It is a common-sense principle that if a pass would be forcing a double is for penalties, unless a specific arrangement is made to the contrary. If North has the intelligence to pass the double of 2♠, East will have to run to 3♡, and now the gambit may well backfire as West is likely to sacrifice in 7♡ over 6♠, losing 1300.

4. Bidding after a take-out double

Among those whose misfortune it is to teach bridge for a living, the first lesson on the take-out double is always approached with particular resignation; old hands usually delegate it to an assistant and retire to the bar. The double poses problems for everyone at the table, and before he can practise the use of his new toy the novice has to learn a new set of rules for whichever position he may occupy. In this chapter we consider the action to be taken by each player in turn after the bidding has begun with an opening bid of one of a suit and a take-out double.

A. OPENER'S PARTNER

As we have already noted, the opener's partner actually has more options open as a result of the double. For one thing he is no longer under pressure to bid if he has nothing interesting to say:

♠Q743 ♡J864 ◇A2 ♣753

After an opening 1◇ from your partner you would normally have to bid a subdued 1♡ or 1♠ on this hand, but after the double you are free to pass and should do so – you would not welcome, say, a heart lead against an opposing spade contract, nor would you wish to have your major suit raised in competition. With one less spade and one more club it would be good tactics to bid 1NT, a mild attempt to pre-empt opponents out of their spade fit.

However, the choices confronting you in this position are not straightforward. The simple change-of-suit response is the first source of confusion. This was traditionally played as non-forcing, guaranteeing nothing but a long suit and a misfit – probably a singleton or void in partner's suit. The idea was to protect the opener against a penalty pass. However, this did not have a very high frequency of occurrence, and in any case was as likely to aggravate the situation as to improve it, so that recently it has become quite normal to ignore the double and play simple suit responses as natural and forcing. If you have not discussed the situation with your partner, and it arises at the table, it is certainly safest to assume the bid is forcing.

Neither method seems to us completely satisfactory. The drawbacks of the non-forcing response have already been noted; as for the forcing response, it is sometimes unsatisfactory not to be able to bid a good suit because you do not have the points to venture to the 2-level. For instance:

♠Q7 ♡852 ◇KQ10876 ♣52

After 1♠-Dbl, is this good enough for a forcing 2◇? Not really . . . yet it is surely desirable to make the bid for tactical reasons.

Looking ahead a little, we should at this point consider the meaning of a jump change of suit. This too is traditionally non-forcing, showing a good 6-card suit in a moderate hand – something like:

♠QJ10964 ♡82 ◇105 ♣A73

After 1◇-Dbl, a bid of 2♠ on this hand is both constructively safe and tactically valuable. However, this interpretation too could create a difficulty on hands such as this:

♠AQJ753 ♡A9 ◇64 ♣AQ6

If 2♠ is non-forcing in the sequence given, what are you supposed to do with this giant? In theory, you redouble first and bid spades later, but it has been known for the opener to be left to play in 1◇ redoubled, making a large score but less than you would have done in 6♠ or 7♠!

The solution to these problems, for regular partnerships, seems to lie in a compromise: a new suit at the 1-level is forcing, and may be bid on a 4-card suit as usual, but a new suit at the 2-level – with or without a jump – is non-forcing, showing a good suit but not very much outside. This seems to get the best of all worlds. Reconsidering the three hands shown above, for instance, on the first you can bid 2♦ and on the second 2♠ facing an opening bid in any other suit and an intervening double. On the third hand, the spade rock-crusher, you kick off with a forcing 1♠; this will cause no more problems later than the traditional redoubling treatment, as some sort of force should always be available. If the opener's partner begins with a one-level force and then makes a further forcing bid on the next round, the inference is clear – the hand is too good in terms of distribution to redouble.

Finally, of course, if you hold a very powerful hand with a big suit which is lower-ranking than partner's you can make a forcing jump shift at the 3-level, effectively ignoring the double:

♠A9 ♡KQJ753 ◇A86 ♣K6

After one of a minor from partner and a double on your right, bid a forcing 1♡, but if the opening bid was 1♠, bid 3♡.

A response of 1NT over the double is normal, showing about 6-9 points and a balanced hand. The inference that you cannot bid a suit at the 1-level is not nearly as strong as it is without the double. Holding:

♠73 ♡Q864 ◇K95 ♣J732

after the bidding starts 1◇-Dbl, it is a better move to respond 1NT than 1♡. For one thing, it may shut out the spades; and in any case, partners who open 1 ◇ are less likely to hold hearts as well.

The redouble of a take-out double, formerly the first move on all hands of about 9 points upwards, tends now to be reserved mainly for those hands with an active interest in defence. The message is that responder has a useful all-round hand, with not more than 3 cards in his partner's suit and good defence to at least two of the other suits; he would like to be given a free hand to take whatever action he thinks best on the next round. An ideal redouble of 1♡ looks like this:

♠Q1097 ♡3 ◇AJ86 ♣KQ95

Clearly you expect to be able to tread heavily on whatever suit opponents escape to, and you would not be pleased to hear partner soldiering on with 2♡ after a suit bid on your left. The redouble in effect says, 'Hands off – this one's mine.' The opener should only bid again in defiance of his partner's request if his hand is clearly sub-standard in terms of defensive potential (see p.63).

It may be necessary to point out that it does not matter whether your partner can make his redoubled contract or not! Unless opponents are incompetent (in which case they will probably let you make it whether it is makable or not) partner *cannot* be left in his contract. The doubler will never be able to pass, as his trumps cannot be good enough; and a pass by the doubler's partner is not for penalties, but merely says he has nothing to offer so far as choice of suit is concerned.

All raises of your partner's suit after the double are essentially defensive. A reasonable yardstick is that if you have 4-card support in the distributional hand you should bid one more than you would have done without the double.

(a) ♠J953	(b) ♠Q875	(c) ♠KJ95
♡6	♡93	♡7
◇97532	◇A7643	◇QJ842
♣986	♣107	♣Q107

After 1♠-Dbl, bid 2♠ on (a), 3♠ on (b) and 4♠ on (c). Without the double, the correct bids are of course No Bid, 2♠ and 3♠ respectively. Obviously this idea should be tempered with a little discretion if vulnerable, but it is worth noting that with most good pairs now using responsive doubles it is not easy for opponents to organize a penalty when you do over-reach.

The final option for third hand in standard bidding is the 2NT response. The type of hand on which you would bid a natural 2NT in this position is an ideal one for the redouble, so the bid is given a conventional meaning. It confirms a sound raise of partner's suit to at least three, with defensive tricks.

(a) ♠64	(b) ♠87
♡KQ93	♡A9542
◇AJ8	◇KJ7
♣J1075	♣KQ9

After a 1 ♥ opening and a double, bid 2NT on both hands, with the first making no further effort over a sign-off of 3 ♥ and with the second pushing on to game. Note that in both cases you would be glad to hear partner making a penalty double of an opposing 4 ♠; this useful convention should stop him sacrificing in a doubtful cause. The direct raise on the other hand promises nothing in defence and implies willingness to sacrifice if the opener sees fit.

Some partnerships use a bid of 3NT over the double to show a hand such as (b) above – a sound raise to game in partner's major – using 2NT to show a raise to precisely 3 of the suit. And a few avant-garde experts have started using a bid of 1NT over the double to show a sound raise to the 2-level. Both these ideas are quite playable: the 3NT response is idle in any natural sense, and 1NT can be replaced by a pass without serious disadvantage.

To conclude this section, we should repeat the warning that this seat is a favourite one for psychic bids, and any bid at all in this position should be regarded as suspect. Change-of-suit responses on xxx and a 3-count, redoubles on shapely Yarboroughs and conventional 2NTs with four small and an outside Jack are all popular amusements. When you suspect someone is pulling your leg in this way, start with a penalty double – anything else may lead to dangerous misunderstandings and an embarrassing disaster.

B.   THE DOUBLER'S PARTNER

Players often experience difficulty in selecting the correct response to a take-out double, yet the theory is simple enough. Again we shall take the most common responses in order, and consider what hand-types they should describe.

Minimum suit responses are the weakest possible calls, in effect merely indicating preference for one of the suits in which the doubler has implied tolerance. They express neither strength nor assurance of suit quality. It is not often that you are given such a free rein to bid whatever you like. After the bidding has started: 1 ♥-Dbl-No, what do you bid with each of the following hands?

(a) ♠10754   (b) ♠J7   (c) ♠Q86
♡J53   ♡532   ♡532
◇43   ◇10832   ◇10843
♣10532   ♣6532   ♣532

With each of them you may feel that your card-holding gives cause for complaint, but you still have to bid something. On hand (a) you bid 1♠, saying no more than that spades are probably your best suit. On hand (b) 2♣ is a more economical choice than 2◇, leaving room for a retreat if a squall blows. On hand (c) it is perhaps better to respond 1♠, keeping the bidding low, than to make the space-consuming response of 2◇. Remember that your partner should be prepared for a 1♠ response, and will accept that you have to make it on a 3-card suit from time to time. It is only right to add that these 3-card responses can lead to disaster even in expert hands, and should be used only when no other choice is remotely possible. As for the doubler, he should proceed with caution when partner has made a minimum response in the cheapest available suit – however gigantic his support, he should continue with a cue-bid rather than a majestic leap to game, and if his partner shows no interest he should give up.

The maximum range for a change-of-suit response at the minimum level is two tricks with a 4-card suit or one and a half with a 5-card suit. These requirements are not totally binding, and you should use your judgement, asking yourself whether a game may be missed if you make a minimum response and partner cannot find a further bid. With this hand:

♠AQ743 ♡632 ◇74 ♣1073

after 1◇-Dbl-No, it is enough to bid 1♠ despite having the technical requirements for a stronger bid. You will not have a good play for game unless partner has at least something like this:

♠K652 ♡97 ◇AQ83 ♣AK6

and with as much as that he will raise 1♠ to 2♠, in which case you can push on.

No-trump responses for the most part show satisfactory guards in opener's suit. For a jump response, a double guard is expected. The real criterion must be that your hand facing what you expect from partner should afford the combined values for the level at which you respond. In principle, the 1NT response therefore suggests 6-9 points, but if the opening bid was in a major it may be necessary to improvise a little and bid 1NT on as little as 4 points. After the bidding has started 1♠-Dbl-No, it would be correct to respond 1NT with any of the following hands:

(a)	♠Q1073	(b)	♠K83	(c)	♠QJ9
	♡K74		♡974		♡974
	◇Q73		◇Q753		◇8753
	♣974		♣A74		♣J74

It is also worth remarking that you should never prefer a 1NT response to a natural bid in a major. An inexperienced player who held this hand in a pairs tournament obtained a very bad result with a bid which at first sight seems not unreasonable:

$$♠KJ98 \quad ♡Q1054 \quad ◇742 \quad ♣98$$

After 1♠-Dbl-No, she bid 1NT, and found her partner with:

$$♠3 \quad ♡A876 \quad ◇A965 \quad ♣KQ73$$

He could not bid again over 1NT, which went one light, with 2♡ makable. Remember that unless the doubler is strong he will always be prepared for the other major, but not necessarily for no trumps.

The bid of 2NT is a limited response showing about 10-12 high-card points. This may seem a little light for the bid, but it is important to bear in mind that a game can often be made on slightly thin values when most of the missing high cards are marked in one defending hand. Some caution is recommended, in case the double is a little shaded because of good distribution. Once again the bid should not be made if it risks missing a major-suit game:

(a) ♠KJ3　　　　　　　(b) ♠KJ3
　　♡74　　　　　　　　　♡AQJ7
　　◇AQJ7　　　　　　　◇74
　　♣10974　　　　　　　♣10974

After 1♠-Dbl-No, with hand (a) there is no sensible alternative to 2NT, with a minor-suit game remote and hearts not in contention. On hand (b) 2NT would be quite wrong, as partner holding:

♠74　♡K986　◇AK32　♣A85

will raise you to 3NT, which has no play even on a spade lead.

You *can* bid 3NT in response to the double on very balanced hands that cannot envisage any other possible contract, but most such hands are better launched with a cue-bid, described below, and 3NT can be more profitably used to describe a hand with a trick in opponents' suit and a long minor of your own that you hope to run:

♠QJ5　♡K8　◇KQJ952　♣65

After 1♠-Dbl-No, this is the sort of hand that justifies a 3NT response.

The minimum requirements for a jump response in a new suit merge with the maximum criteria for a simple response. With a 5-card suit, a minimum is one and a half quick tricks; with only a 4-card suit you need enough to have raised this suit to the 3-level if partner had opened it.

(a) ♠KJ854　　　　　　(b) ♠AKJ5
　　♡74　　　　　　　　　♡974
　　◇A1054　　　　　　　◇54
　　♣84　　　　　　　　　♣Q842

After 1♣-Dbl-No, bid 2♠ on either of these hands.

A double jump in a new suit shows a weak hand with a useful 6- or 7-card suit. After 1♡-Dbl-No, this hand is a typical jump to 3♠:

♠QJ86432　♡542　◇J　♣106

A jump to game is made on a similar hand with a trick outside, offering no great slam potential. After the bidding 1♡-Dbl-No, jump to 4♠ with:

♠KQ10852 ♡K6 ◇10742 ♣2

but with a hand as good as:

♠AK8532 ♡A74 ◇4 ♣Q82

start with a cue-bid to investigate the considerable slam chances.

The cue-bid of opponents' suit in response to a take-out double is often employed on very moderate values in the modern game. It denotes either a hand with at least one and a half tricks which can offer a choice of suits, or a strong hand which needs plenty of bidding-space to discover the full potential of the partnership values. As so often, the cue-bid is a useful general-purpose bid which keeps the fire burning while the doubler describes his hand. Here is an example of the expert use of the cue-bid which occurred in a high-stake rubber game in London. With South the dealer at Game All, West held:

♠AQ4 ♡54 ◇AK73 ♣KQ72

and doubled an opening 1♡ on his right. East had:

♠K953 ♡92 ◇QJ106 ♣A65

and made a cue-bid of 2♡, a better bid than 2♠ with a not very robust spade suit and obvious alternatives available if spades proved unsatisfactory. This cue-bid is normally played as forcing to suit-agreement only, not to game. West now bid 3♡, a second cue-bid passing the buck back to his partner, and establishing a game-forcing situation. When East bid 3♠ West was able to judge that the suit was relatively poor, so he bid 4♣. East now showed his diamonds, and the partnership duly reached the lay-down diamond game.

The final option open to the doubler's partner after a pass on his right is a penalty pass. You should think very carefully before taking this step . . . and having thought about it you should normally reject it. The pass is correct at teams or rubber bridge only when no better spot is likely to be available:

♠64 ♡97 ◇QJ10863 ♣752

After 1 ◇-Dbl-No, this is the rare type of hand on which to pass for penalties. However exotic partner's double may be, he is unlikely to make anything facing such a dummy; and, while you will not always beat 1 ◇ doubled, defending against it will surely prove the best course of action. Except at duplicate pairs, where it may pay to pass on less suitable hands, the penalty pass should be made with reluctance, not enthusiasm. After all, your partner is not going to get a chance to bid again, and he may have an Acol Two bid in one of the other suits, with a void in the prospective trump suit.

We have so far considered only those situations in which the opener's partner has passed over the double. If instead he bids something, the position is rather different. The doubler's partner is now free to pass on minimum hands, so that any bid from him is assumed to show some values. However, you should still make a jump response when the hand justifies one. With a holding such as:

$$\spadesuit AQ963 \quad \heartsuit 75 \quad \diamondsuit QJ3 \quad \clubsuit 852$$

after the bidding has started 1 ♡-Dbl-2♣, it may be tempting to bid a lazy 2♠, reasoning that as you did not have to bid at all partner should place you with a fair hand. But you would also bid 2♠ in this position on:

$$\spadesuit J10853 \quad \heartsuit 6 \quad \diamondsuit QJ42 \quad \clubsuit 954$$

hoping to stop opener rebidding his hearts and steal the contract at a low level. With a good 5-card suit and a couple of tricks, therefore, you should still make a jump response even after the bid on your right.

The cue-bid too can still be used, but it should always be made in the suit bid by opener. For one thing, this will always be the lower of the two possible bids; also, as we have seen, third hand's suit is quite often imaginary, and it is useful to have a natural bid available in that suit. Consider the following two hands:

(a)	♠KQ106	(b)	♠KQ9873
	♡A74		♡J65
	◇932		◇632
	♣875		♣4

After the bidding 1♣-Dbl-1♠, with hand (a) you should double for penalties – the spade suit may be genuine, and your hand is primarily a defensive type. Hand (b) is another matter entirely – you can be almost certain that the spade bidder is messing about, no doubt with club support in reserve, and a double here would be quite wrong. A bid of 2♠ describes your hand, and will unambiguously unmask the psychist; after a double, you may have trouble persuading partner how good your spades are.

In general, then, you should tend to ignore a change-of-suit bid on your right. This also applies if you want to bid no trumps – you must have an adequate guard in the opener's suit, but you promise nothing in his partner's. Holding:

$$\spadesuit QJ86 \quad \heartsuit A95 \quad \diamondsuit K86 \quad \clubsuit 752$$

after the bidding 1♠-Dbl-2♣, you should bid 2NT. Your partner probably has the clubs held himself, but in any case he should not rely on you for them.

We conclude this section with an examination of one of the best-established modern aids to competitive bidding, the Responsive Double.

A responsive double is a conventional double of a supported suit in response to partner's take-out double. In both the following sequences, the double may by arrangement be played as responsive:

> (a) 1♡-Dbl-2♡-Dbl
> (b) 1♣-Dbl-3♣-Dbl

The requirements for this call are length in at least two of the unbid suits, and the values to enter the bidding at the appropriate level. Notice how closely this compares with the requirements for a normal take-out double – the desire to compete without the ability to suggest a trump suit. Here are three examples of the responsive double in action:

(a)	(b)	(c)
♠J74	♠KQ74	♠K1096
♡75	♡852	♡74
◇AJ74	◇QJ74	◇AQJ3
♣QJ62	♣62	♣853

With (a), after 1♡-Dbl-2♡, you have the ideal hand for a responsive double. If partner bids 2♠, the hand should play well enough even in a 4-3 fit, as your hand will be able to take heart ruffs; and three of either minor should obviously be a secure contract. With (b), after the same bidding, the responsive double is still correct: if partner bids 3♣ you go to 3◇, showing the spades by implication, and if the doubler has the worst possible shape for you, 3-3-2-5, he can now convert to 3♠ (or 3NT if he holds the hearts). Again the 4-3 spade fit should be playable, as partner should have considerable extra values when he has doubled on such poor shape. With hand (c), after 1♣-Dbl-3♣, you have values to justify a bid at the 3-level, and a choice of possible trump-suits, so again you double. If partner bids the missing suit, 3♡, you go 3♠, and whether partner passes or raises you should be in a good contract.

It is worth considering how the responsive double conforms to the theory concerning conventional bids. On natural methods, you have a problem with this hand:

$$♠753 \quad ♡K1094 \quad ◇AQ75 \quad ♣74$$

when the bidding in front of you goes 1♠-Dbl-2♠. This hand clearly merits action at the 3-level. Once it was entirely acceptable to call 3♡, safe in the knowledge that partner would hold either a 4-card heart suit or a strong hand. However, the modern informatory double does not make such positive guarantees – partner could hold:

$$♠Q6 \quad ♡AQ8 \quad ◇K965 \quad ♣QJ108$$

in which case 3♡ may well prove to be one too many, whereas 3◇ is safe. Playing responsive doubles, you are in no difficulty with these hands: you double, partner bids 3♣, and when you bid 3◇, showing diamonds and hearts, your partner will know it is time to stop.

This hand from a recent pairs tournament shows how the responsive double can solve the problems caused by aggressive pre-emptive action from opponents. North held, at Love All:

$$♠AQ76 \quad ♡A2 \quad ◇KQ9853 \quad ♣6$$

and doubled an opening 1♡ bid on his right. At several tables a raise to 3♡ now set an awkward problem for South, who held:

♠KJ83 ♡K5 ◊2 ♣Q109832

When South bid a natural 4♣, and West continued to 4♡, North felt unable to bid 4♠ on his 4-card suit, and either doubled for a disappointing penalty or bid 5◊, going down. Where North-South were playing responsive doubles, however, the solid spade game was easily reached.

As always, when borrowing a bid for conventional purposes, you must be happy that you are not leaving a larger gap else-where. The animal that is now left homeless is this one:

♠K10985 ♡74 ◊A84 ♣753

After 1♠-Dbl-2♠, you may wish you could double for penal-ties, but there is really nothing wrong with passing (or, with a queen more, perhaps calling 2NT). It may not produce your best result, but neither will it ever lead to a ridiculous one. In any event, even if you could double for penalties it might well be less lucrative than you expect – partner probably has no trump to lead, and declarer may come to quite a lot of tricks on a cross-ruff. Finally, of course, the more enticing your penalty double looks, the more likely partner is to take it out!

The other side of the coin is that the responsive double often gives opportunities for penalties in situations where natural bidding does not even come close to collecting anything.

Dealer South, Game All

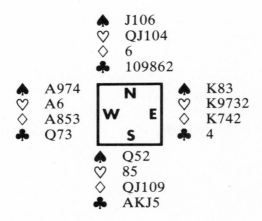

	♠	J106
	♡	QJ104
	◊	6
	♣	109862

♠	A974		♠	K83
♡	A6		♡	K9732
◊	A853		◊	K742
♣	Q73		♣	4

	♠	Q52
	♡	85
	◊	QJ109
	♣	AKJ5

In both rooms the first three bids were the same: 1♣ from South, Double from West and a pre-emptive 3♣ from North. In Room 1, East-West were not playing responsive doubles, and East had to bid 3♡; West could not safely take any further action, and East took only seven tricks, losing 200. In Room 2, East made a responsive double of 3♣, and West, with good defensive tricks, poor suits of his own and a ruffing-value in clubs, elected to pass for penalties. This type of action will occasionally lead to an embarrassing −470 or −530 (scores familiar to the duplicate enthusiast), but these setbacks should be amply compensated for by all the +300s and +500s on part-score hands.

It is difficult to limit the responsive double in terms of high-card points, especially as the level to which the auction may go can depend on the suit the original doubler chooses. For instance, suppose you hold:

♠Q853 ♡63 ◇KJ852 ♣84

and the bidding in front of you goes 1♡-Dbl-2♡. This hand is just good enough for a responsive double – partner is likely to have 4 cards in spades, but if the bidding does go to the 3-level you at least have a 5-card suit as compensation for the slim values.

The limits on distribution are equally hard to define. The important thing to remember is that the double says you are unable to select a trump suit. As possession of a good 5-card or longer major is sufficient cause to bid that suit in response to a double, a responsive double should in principle deny such a holding. This is a point that the original doubler should bear in mind. Suppose you hold:

♠AK7 ♡74 ◇Q63 ♣KQ753

After an opening 1♡ on your right you decide to double; next hand raises to 2♡, and your partner's responsive double is passed to you. You bid 3♣, and partner says 3◇. Your immediate reaction might be to give preference to partner's known spade suit. However, the right bid is to pass: partner should hold exactly 4 spades, whereas his diamonds may be a 5-card suit. Indeed, he may hold the hand shown in the last example.

C. THE OPENER

There is rather less that needs to be said about the opener's second turn. In general he should proceed with caution, as the hand on his left may be very strong:

♠A64 ♡KJ93 ◇AQJ72 ♣6

After 1◇-Dbl-No-1♠, there is no point in bidding again on this hand. To do so simply offers opponents the option of defending, and will not inconvenience them. If the doubler passes the 1♠ bid your partner is still there, and will now know that you have a sound opening, so that he will surely compete if necessary.

♠A93 ♡K9 ◇AQJ732 ♣85

This is the sort of hand on which you should bid 2◇ on the second round in the sequence given. This mildly pre-emptive effort will inconvenience the doubler if he has a strong hand with a club suit, and you are telling your partner that your suit is good and your defensive strength limited.

If partner has redoubled, the rules for opener are fairly clear-cut. There are only two situations in which he should bid again: when he has a weak opening very unsuited to defence; and when he can double a bid on his right for penalties. In other cases you should respect partner's redouble as a request to leave the next round to him.

(a) ♠64	(b) ♠73	(c) ♠AJ43
♡AK8753	♡AQ9852	♡KJ8643
◇A93	◇–	◇Q7
♣108	♣AK763	♣5

After 1♡-Dbl-Rdbl-1♠, on hand (a) you should pass. It is a mistake to bid 2♡ just because the opening is minimum in terms of point-count – with three defensive tricks you have at least as much as partner can reasonably expect. If partner doubles 1♠ now you should stand it. He may have:

♠K953 ♡2 ◇KJ84 ♣A972

which should be enough to beat 1♠, but you will have difficulty achieving a plus score if you run prematurely to 2♡.

With hand (b) you are unsuited to defence, but it is still better to pass at this stage. If partner doubles 1♠ (or a 2◇ bid by the doubler) you bid your clubs, describing your hand well – a sound opening, but two-suited.

Hand (c) shows the other side of the picture. Many players would be tempted to double 1♠, but this would be unwise as you have no defence to a minor-suit contract. To bid 2♡ after partner has doubled 2♣ or 2◇ would suggest a stronger type of hand such as:

♠AJ95 ♡KQJ872 ◇6 ♣AQ

The best move on hand (c) is to bid 2♡ at once, a clear warning to your partner that any operations he undertakes against the minors will be at his own risk.

A problem that will arise from time to time is how to cope with a penalty pass on your right:

♠AJ3 ♡K72 ◇A843 ♣K105

After 1◇-Dbl-No-No, it is certainly worth trying to escape. Assuming that your opponents know what they are doing, you are about to run into a 6-1 trump break, with most of the high cards sitting over you. Partner must have a suit of some kind, and an SOS redouble will persuade him to mention it. If he has this kind of thing:

♠52 ♡J9643 ◇76 ♣Q942

he may not enjoy himself much in 1♡ doubled, but at least he will make more tricks than you would have done in diamonds. If he has a balanced Yarborough, things can hardly get any worse than they already are. Besides, opponents often misjudge these positions, coming back into the auction or leaving you to play undoubled.

A final small point for the opener to consider is the meaning of a double of a cue-bid. After 1♡-Dbl-No-2♡, a double by the opener is often used to mean no more than, 'Hey, that's *my* suit.' Such futile doubles merely increase the range of bids open to opponents. A double in this position should stress the quality of opener's suit, confirming that he would like it led even if partner has no useful card in it.

D.   THE DOUBLER

Suppose that you are dealt this hand:

♠Q1073   ♡75   ◇AKJ3   ♣K106

and double an opening 1♡ on your right. Next hand passes, and partner bids 1♠, which is passed to you. What do you bid? One of the authors gave this hand as a problem to ten players, all of whom consider themselves above average. Their verdict: 5 votes for 2♠, 2 each for 3♠ and No Bid, and 1 for 4♠.

The correct answer is *No Bid*. The 1♠ response is in effect simply a weak preference, and promises no values whatsoever. After making a take-out double you should pass all minimum suit responses unless you have some additional strength. A useful yardstick when deciding whether to raise partner's suit is this: if he had bid that suit in response to an opening bid by you, would you now be strong enough to jump-raise it? If so, you can give a single raise after a take-out double.

♠AQ75   ♡75   ◇AK62   ♣KQ6

If you open 1◇ on this hand and partner responds 1♠, you raise to 3♠. Therefore after 1♡ on your right, double from you and 1♠ from partner, you are worth a free raise to 2♠. It may not sound very strong, but it is quite enough – remember that partner may have a shapeless Yarborough, and does not even guarantee a 4-card spade suit.

For a double raise of partner's suit, you should have approximately the values for a maximum opening one-bid, with fair distribution. After the same auction (1♡-Dbl-No-1♠), raise to 3♠ with:

♠AKJ6   ♡6   ◇KQ742   ♣AJ10

Before making the double raise you should be sure that no alternative strain can be better: with this hand:

♠AJ85   ♡A6   ◇AQJ10   ♣KQ7

it is better to start with a cue-bid of 2♡ after the auction given, as the hand may play better in another spot than it does in spades. Give partner this holding:

♠K63 ♡Q72 ◇8532 ♣J62

on which he might well elect to reply 1♠ to your double, and it is easy to see that 3NT is a far better proposition than 4♠. With that hand, in fact, partner should jump to 3NT over your cue-bid – both his overall strength and his heart holding are as good as you can possibly expect.

A change of suit by the doubler indicates a better than minimum double, and in principle shows a 5-card suit. (Not however a 6-card suit, as on such a hand you should have preferred a jump overcall to a double in the first place.) After 1♡-Dbl-No-1♠, a bid of 2♣ by the doubler at his second turn shows something like:

♠A62 ♡9 ◇KQJ7 ♣AQ764

The 4-card holding in the unbid suit (diamonds here) is not essential but is quite likely. It is important to note that the change of suit is normally non-forcing, but becomes forcing if partner has made a jump suit bid in response to your original take-out double.

A jump in a new suit can be made on a hand which would qualify for the one-suited variety of Acol Two bid; the two-suited type, and any bigger hand, should be introduced with a direct cue-bid of opponents' suit. The jump is not completely forcing, therefore, and responder may pass if he does not expect his hand to contribute a trick. There is no implication that the doubler has support for any other suit, and if responder insists on his own suit he should be prepared to play in it opposite a singleton.

If the responder to the double had bid no trumps, further bidding by the doubler is entirely natural. If he bids a suit over a 1NT response, this should be construed as mildly constructive but non-forcing. Any other suit bid – a jump over 1NT, or any suit bid over a higher no-trump response – is forcing, looking for an alternative contract.

A rebid in no trumps by the doubler shows a hand too strong to overcall 1NT on the first round. There are no hard and fast rules about the point-count required for various no-trump rebids, but the following is an approximate guide.

1) If partner has made a simple suit response at the one-level, a rebid of 1NT shows 18-20 points, 2NT 21-22. With more than that it is better to cue-bid first. A jump to 3NT in this position will rarely be a safe move without a very good suit to run.

2) If the response was at the 2-level, opener has a more difficult decision: partner may still be very weak, but there is too little room for manoeuvre. It is safe to bid 2NT on hands of 20 points upwards, but with less than that it is wiser to look for an alternative, such as a cue-bid (which will always be available at the 2-level) or possibly a raise of partner's minor.

3) If partner has made a jump response, or has bid freely over intervention by opener's partner, the simplest approach is to treat a 2NT rebid by the doubler as forcing, showing any strength from 18 points upward.

As usual, when you have a good hand which does not fit neatly into any of the categories described above, a cue-bid of opponents' suit is available to ask partner to describe his hand further. After you have doubled an opening 1♡ on your right, and your partner's 2♣ response has been passed to you, a cue-bid of 2♡ is the best move on any of the following hands:

	(a)	(b)	(c)
	♠AK5	♠KQ743	♠KQ64
	♡6	♡A	♡J73
	◇A753	◇AQJ109	◇AKJ6
	♣KQJ84	♣Q6	♣AQ

On hand (a) you have excellent support for clubs, but need room to explore further before making any decisions. With hand (b) you are too strong for a non-forcing 2◇ or 2♠, whereas a jump in either suit would suggest a one-suited hand – a forcing 2♡ should eventually persuade partner to choose between your suits. Hand (c) may offer a play for 3NT if partner can supply a bolster in hearts. The cue-bid is once again required to bear quite a heavy load, but the next round of bidding usually makes things clear.

In all the cases we have looked at so far in this section, the doubler's partner has made the previous bid. When the opener bids on the second round, or a bid by your left-hand opponent has been passed back to you, further bidding is natural. The only doubtful instance is when the doubler doubles again: here the principle is that doubles of no trumps or of new suits are for penalties, but a second double of the original suit is not. The meaning of this double depends on whether the doubler's partner has bid. In this sequence:

1♡	Dbl	2♡	No
No	Dbl		

the doubler is simply making a further attempt to get his partner to say something – probably the double is based on a good three-suited hand. Rather different is this type of sequence:

1♡	Dbl	No	1♠
2♡	Dbl		

If we apply the traditional rule of thumb, this is a penalty double for two reasons: partner has bid, and the doubler is doubling a rebid unsupported suit. One might possibly want to make a penalty double in this position, perhaps with such a hand as:

$$♠A5 \quad ♡KQ108 \quad ◇AJ96 \quad ♣AQ2$$

that is, a hand strong in the enemy suit which was too good to bid 1NT on the first round. However, this is an uneconomical use: you are as likely to get a good score by making your planned rebid of 2NT, and in any case it is unlikely that the opener will bid again without a strong suit, so you will rarely hold such a hand in this position. A more useful purpose for the double here is to play it as 'competitive', showing a hand which would have raised freely to 2♠ had the opener passed; this allows you to bid 2♠ on weaker hands simply to contest the part-score.

5. Artificial intervention

The modern game has produced a number of interesting artificial or semi-artificial conventions for the defending side, making use of some largely idle bids to describe certain types of distributional hands. In this chapter we examine some of the more popular and valuable of these gadgets as used over opening bids of one of a suit, 1NT or an artificial 1♣.

A. THE TRADITIONAL CUE-BID

The most obviously idle bid after a natural opening of one of a suit is the immediate overcall in the same suit. Standard practice is to treat this bid as equivalent to an Acol 2♣ opening. Contrary to popular belief, however, the cue-bid should show not merely a hand which is too strong for a take-out double, but one which *cannot* safely be introduced with a double because of the risk of a penalty pass. In practice, this means that the cue-bid should be reserved for very strong one-suited or two-suited hands. The following hands would both justify a cue-bid after a minor-suit opening:

(a) ♠AKQJ854   (b) ♣KQJ1085
    ♡KQ5   ♡AKJ105
    ◇5   ◇A
    ♣A4   ♣4

A Stone Age view insists that the cue-bid guarantees first-round control of the enemy suit, but this is no longer a tenable concept today.

B. MICHAELS CUE-BIDS

Many expert players now accept that the traditional cue-bid gives poor value for money: it occurs too infrequently, and the hands it shows can be bid in another way. The most popular alternative uses for the cue-bid are the Michaels version and the integrated system of overcalls devised by Pierre Ghestem and used in several European bidding systems.

The Michaels idea as usually played today allocates a varying meaning to the cue-bid, depending on the suit involved.

Over 1♣ or 1◇ it shows a major two-suiter (at least 5-4), and in theory a weak hand with 6-10 high-card points. With this hand:

♠Q9643   ♡AJ876   ◇53   ♣2

after an opening 1♣ or 1◇ on your right it is obviously a great advantage to be able to show both suits with a single bid. In fact it is doubtful whether the hand justifies an overcall at all if not playing Michaels – to bid 1♠ on such a poor suit is unattractive, while 1♡ lacks pre-emptive value and in any case may lead to the wrong contract.

Over 1♡ the cue-bid shows a weak take-out double with 5 cards in spades and at least tolerance for both minors. If you hold:

♠QJ964   ♡7   ◇AJ32   ♣Q96

an overcall of 1♠ over 1♡ would be unsatisfactory on a hand which will play well in any of three suits, and a take-out double (unless you have previously passed) would be quite unsound.

Over 1♠ the cue-bid is used to show a two-suited hand with hearts and one of the minors. As partner is going to have to bid at the level of three, this version can only be safely used on genuine two-suited hands with at least 5-5 in the suits.

♠–   ♡KJ1053   ◇76   ♣K108642

If not playing Michaels you would have a problem with this hand after an opening 1♠ on your right – a 2♡ overcall is out of the question, and 2♣ might even result in a missed game, apart from being tactically futile.

Only one artificial aid is required by the responder to the

Michaels bid: after the 2♠ cue-bid he can bid 2NT to inquire which is partner's minor. In other cases the cue-bid has adequately described the hand, and partner should be able to take control.

There are two further points to make regarding this excellent convention. First, even if you are reluctant to abandon the old-style heavyweight cue-bid, it costs nothing to play the Michaels version after passing. None of the example hands given above has a sound opening bid, but all need a satisfactory way of entering the auction after a fourth-hand bid on the right. Also, provided the cue-bid is played as unconditionally forcing, it is possible to use it as a two-way bid, so that big distributional hands can still be launched with a cue-bid. However, this should be done only when the distribution of the big hand corresponds to what partner will expect from a normal Michaels bid. Look back at the two example hands given in the section on the traditional cue-bid: hand (b) can still be introduced with a pseudo-Michaels cue-bid after 1♣ or 1◇, telling partner about the two suits immediately and taking violent action later to express the unexpected power of the hand. With hand (a), however, this course of action would be unsafe, as you may find it hard to convince your partner that your 'two-suiter' is a 7-3 one! On hand (a) you would have to choose between an immediate 4♠, perhaps missing a slam, and a take-out double, taking the very slight risk that it may be passed out. On balance, the Michaels cue-bid gains far more than it loses, and deserves its increasing popularity.

Ghestem Overcalls
The scheme of jump overcalls and cue-bids incorporated by Pierre Ghestem and René Bacherich in their Monaco Relay system has survived the system itself. These bids were later included in the Blue Club, and are quite widely used in British tournament play. The idea is simple enough: after an opening bid of 1◇, 1♡ or 1♠, an overcall of 2NT shows the lower-ranking two suits (exactly as with the Unusual No Trump), 3♣ shows the two suits other than clubs, and a cue-bid the remaining pair of suits, the extremes. The original version was that over a 1♣ opening 2◇ showed the majors, 2NT the red suits and 3♣ spades and diamonds, the idea being that 1♣ was so often an

artificial opening that a natural 2♣ overcall was needed. This is less true in Britain than in France, however, and some British players prefer to bid 2♣ to show a major two-suiter.

Like the Unusual No Trump, the Ghestem overcall is essentially a constructive bid, showing at least 10 cards in the suits and something in the region of 5 losers. To reduce these standards is greatly to diminish the efficiency of the bid. Correct use of the convention produced a massive swing on this deal from an early round of the 1978 Gold Cup:

Dealer West, North-South Game

```
                    ♠ AKJ964
                    ♡ 10
                    ♢ KJ1065
                    ♣ A
        ♠ 7              N              ♠ 108532
        ♡ AQJ8                          ♡ K97654
        ♢ Q74        W       E          ♢ —
        ♣ QJ863          S              ♣ K9
                    ♠ Q
                    ♡ 32
                    ♢ A9832
                    ♣ 107542
```

	West	North	East	South
Room 1	1♣	Dbl	2♡	No
	4♡	4♠	Dbl	No
	5♡	No	No	Dbl
	No	No	No	
Room 2	1♣	3♣	No	4♢
	No	4NT	No	5♢
	No	6♢	No	No
	No			

The bidding in Room 1 is a good example of the difficulties involved in handing two-suited hands with a take-out double. East felt pleased to have pushed his opponents into 4♠, but West judged well to remove the double, aware that his partner might expect more defensive tricks than he had. In Room 2 the Ghestem overcall of 3♣ showed a strong diamond-spade two-suiter, enabling South to take a very rosy view of his 5-card diamond suit and his ♠Q.

It is possible to use Ghestem overcalls on weak hands after passing, but this is not very efficient – a combination of the Unusual No Trump and Michaels works better. The main disadvantage of the method is the loss of 3♣ as a normal strong jump overcall, but in practice these rare birds can be managed comfortably enough with a take-out double.

C.   THE UNUSUAL NO TRUMP

Few modern conventions have been as widely accepted as the Unusual No Trump, which is used (or, more likely, abused) by almost all British tournament players. The original idea was that a bid of no trumps which could not possibly be genuine showed a pronounced two-suiter in the unbid suits, or the lower two suits if only one had been bid. The most easily recognizable case occurs when a player who has previously passed enters the auction with a no-trump overcall:

North	East	South	West
No	No	No	1♡
1NT			

Clearly the 1NT bid here is useless in any natural sense. Using the convention, North shows a minor two-suiter, and values just short of an opening bid. This however is not one of the most valuable uses of the convention: two passed hands with strength in the minors are almost certain to be outbid, and the 1NT bid will merely warn declarer that he can expect bad breaks. A further point is that East-West may well have a misfit, and if left to themselves may run into trouble. So the bid in this position should be kept well up to strength, about 9-10 points and a genuine 5-5 two-suiter.

This sequence is different:

North	East	South	West
No	No	No	1♡
No	No	1NT	

Here South's bid is a normal protective no trump, showing about 10-11 points in a balanced hand and hoping to contest the part-score. With this hand:

♠64   ♡7   ◇KJ953   ♣KQ863

South might venture 2NT, hoping to buy the contract in 3 of a minor.

The convention was extended early in its history to include an immediate overcall of 2NT, a bid which is not strictly idle in a natural sense, but would occur rarely. This is the case in which the Unusual No Trump is most often abused. An immediate 2NT overcall should be a constructive bid, made on a two-suited hand of good quality which has reasonable expectations of buying the contract. Even at favourable vulnerability it should be no worse than:

♠3   ♡A10   ◇KJ1084   ♣KQ753

and at other vulnerability conditions an extra trick is desirable. To come lurching in with 2NT over 1♡ on:

♠2   ♡–   ◇976532   ♣K98542

is suicidal. The player who deemed this hand worthy of an Unusual 2NT in a multiple teams event finished up losing 1700 (not vulnerable, at that!), which was precisely what he might have expected. His opposite number at the other table passed on the first round, and was very glad he had when the bidding started 1♡-2♣-3◇, to subside eventually in 5♡, which proved to be one too many against the appalling and unexpected breaks.

The most valuable uses of the Unusual No Trump are the less obvious ones. In this sequence:

North	East	South	West
1♠	2♣	2♠	No
No	2NT		

East has shown a hand of this kind:

♠10 ♡A6 ◇QJ87 ♣AQ7432

where 2NT is a much more helpful effort than a unilateral 3♣. (To bid 2NT on the first round is of course revolting, though some would do it – the suits *must* be of comparable quality.) Similarly:

North	East	South	West
1◇	No	No	1♠
Dbl	2♠	2NT	

South has a weak heart-club two-suiter, and is prepared to contest the part-score now that he has heard his partner announce values outside diamonds.

Another sequence of the same type which is well worth remembering is this one:

North	East	South	West
1◇	1♠	No	4♠
4NT			

where the 4NT carries the message of excellent diamonds and a fragile 4-card club suit. (With better clubs, of course, one could bid 5♣.)

One situation that can lead to misunderstandings is this:

North	East	South	West
1◇	No	1♠	1NT

Clearly it is not impossible for West to hold a strong balanced hand with solid guards in diamonds and spades . . . but if he has such a hand, this is surely the wrong moment to say so! If South's response had taken the bidding to the 2-level, the natural interpretation would be even more unlikely. It is much more sensible to play this bid as 'Unusual', allowing West to bid 1NT on:

♠98 ♡KQ752 ◇3 ♣AJ1064

enabling him to differentiate between this genuine two-suiter and a more balanced type of hand with defensive prospects, such as:

♠AJ8 ♡KQ75 ◇KJ94 ♣Q2

where a normal take-out double is appropriate. Similarly, if South had raised his partner's opening, 2NT should still be played as unusual.

In the right hands, the Unusual No Trump is a very valuable aid to competitive bidding, making use of idle bids to pass messages to partner in considerable detail. Like Blackwood, however, it seems addictive; players trot it out on all sorts of unsuitable hands with the fervour of an alcoholic downing his breakfast gin. Make sure that the bid will say exactly what you want it to, and that the information will be more use to your own side than to your opponents.

D.   DEFENDING AGAINST 1NT

It says something for the pre-emptive value of a 1NT opening that a large number of conventions have been devised to counter it, yet none is entirely satisfactory. The problem is not difficult to see: a 2-level overcall should always be based on a good suit, but if an opponent has opened 1NT in front of you then (a) you are less likely than usual to have a good suit, (b) you are more likely than usual to want to defend if you have got one, and (c) if you reduce the requirements for the overcall the next hand is much better placed than usual to judge when to double. The time when you want to compete is when you have a fair hand playable in two or three suits, and it is for such hands that the weapons examined in this section were developed.

Broadly speaking, defences to 1NT fall into two groups: those which show specifically two-suited hands, and those which purport to show three-suiters. The main representatives of the first group are the Astro family: the original Astro convention; the later development known as Aspro; and the recent hybrid, Asptro. As these are all very similar in intent and effect, we can examine one in detail, and describe the others briefly in terms of how they differ.

Aspro is perhaps the most efficient, though there is little to choose. An overcall of 2♣ shows hearts and any other suit; 2 ◇ shows spades and a minor. The normal requirements are at least 9 cards in the two suits, and a hand not strong enough for a penalty double – an important point, as both overcalls are non-forcing. Like the other overcalls in this group, Aspro requires understanding of a special terminology: the suit promised by the overcaller is the 'anchor major', and the suit immediately above the one actually bid is the 'neutral suit'.

If the responder has a fit for the anchor major he 'raises' it in much the same way as he would an opening one-bid, bearing in mind however that a bid of two of the major promises nothing more than a 3-card fit in what may be a Yarborough.

	(a)	(b)	(c)
♠	7	72	A73
♡	953	Q864	J954
◇	86432	K75	2
♣	9643	KJ85	KJ1032

After 1NT on your left, 2♣ (Aspro) from partner, No Bid on your right, you must bid 2♡ with both (a) and (b). With (a), if you take any other action you are likely to make matters worse by encouraging partner to unveil his spade suit. Hand (b) is a maximum 2♡, but the weakness of the unsupported kings sitting under the no-trump bidder should deter you from anything more ambitious. With hand (c) you would raise an opening 1♡ to 3♡, and so you bid 3♡ here.

With a hand on which you are unwilling or unable to support the anchor major, the usual solution is to bid 2 of the neutral suit.

	(a)	(b)	(c)
♠	75	Q654	842
♡	652	108	9
◇	8643	AJ3	QJ7
♣	9743	K653	K86532

With hand (a) it would be thoughtless to bid 2♡, despite the 3-card fit. A bid of 2◇ keeps the options open: if partner's second suit is diamonds he will pass, and if he has 4 hearts and 5 clubs he will bid 3♣, either of these being a likely improvement on 2♡. With 5 hearts he will bid 2♡ himself, and with 5-4 in the majors 2♠, so that at the worst you have at least improved the chances of playing the hand the right way round. Hand (b) is a more typical 2◇ bid, with no fit for hearts but good prospects anywhere else; if partner rebids his hearts he is likely to have a black suit as his second string, and you can pursue your investigations with 2♠. Hand (c) is the fairly rare case where a pass is correct – a weak hand with 6 cards in the artificial suit and no fit for the anchor major.

In theory the only forcing response to an Aspro overcall is a 'raise' of the artificial suit. However, this idea clearly requires modification. Suppose that you hold:

♠AQ7 ♡8 ◇KJ42 ♣A8753

Left-hand opponent opens 1NT, and partner bids (in the first instance) 2♣. Here the 3♣ force will work well enough. If the Aspro bidder says 3♠, showing 5-4 in the majors, you can raise to 4♠, and if he says 3◇ or 3♡ you can try 3NT. With 4 hearts and 5 clubs he should bid 3NT himself, rather than 4♣.

If partner's overcall was 2◇, however, a raise to 3◇ leaves him awkwardly placed. If he has 4 spades and a 5-card minor he cannot specify his suit without going to the 4-level. This problem is easier to solve than most: as the neutral-suit response of 2♡ over 2◇ is *never* passed (hearts being the one suit the Aspro bidder has specifically denied) you can use it on quite strong hands – any hand, in fact, which has no spade fit but may be playable in 3NT. With a hand such as the one shown you do bid 3◇, and the message now is that you are prepared to go beyond 3NT if necessary. With 5 spades partner bids 3♠, and now you can bid 3NT to ask for the minor. With only 4 cards in spades he bids 3♡ with a single stop in hearts, 3NT with a double stop, or 4 of his minor with nothing in hearts.

Other responses to the Aspro overcall are natural and non-forcing. A bid of a new suit generally shows 6, though 2♠ over 2♣ may be bid with a fair 5-card suit. 2NT shows about 11-13 points and a balanced hand with only a doubleton in the anchor major; if bid in response to 2◇ it should also stress good hearts, as that suit is sure to be led.

Astro differs from Aspro in that 2♣ shows hearts and a minor, 2◇ spades and any other suit. Also, the forcing response is 2NT, and a raise of the bid suit is natural. The loss of a 2NT response in its natural sense is a slight drawback, but perhaps more serious is the increased chance that the Astro bidder will hold the neutral suit. Having overcalled 2◇ on:

♠AQ965 ♡KJ74 ◇103 ♣82

you have an awkward choice when partner bids 2♡. If you pass you may be leaving him in a 4-2 fit when a 5-2 was available; on the other hand to bid 2♠ may mean exchanging a tolerable 4-3 fit for a horrible 5-1.

Asptro is an attempt to get the best of both worlds by always specifying the better major: 2♣ shows hearts and any other suit, 2♢ spades and any other. This has obvious advantages on 5-4 and 4-5 major hands, but it must be doubtful whether these outweigh the loss of definition on major-minor two-suiters.

The other two-suited defence which is occasionally encountered is the one properly known as *Landy* but often described vaguely as 'Stayman'. Here the only conventional overcall is 2♣, which shows the majors. Most published accounts describe a 2♢ response as natural, with long diamonds, but it seems more useful to treat it as a waiting bid, showing equal length in the majors and inviting the 2♣ bidder to choose. The convention is clearly safe enough when the right hand comes along, but its low frequency renders it inferior to the Astro group.

Of the three-suited defences, the most popular is *Sharples*. However, the situation here is complicated by the fact that many players who claim to be using Sharples are in fact following the method correctly known as *Ripstra*! The Sharples convention, as defined in the 1979 Yearbook of the E.B.U. Laws and Ethics Committee, uses a 2♣ overcall as a random take-out on a distributional hand containing at least 4 spades, while 2♢ is similar but promises short clubs. Responses are natural, with 4-card suits being shown in ascending order until a fit is found, and the convention is not used by the player sitting under the 1NT bidder. Sharples has the obvious advantage of flexibility and the equally obvious disadvantage of vagueness: it is safe enough in expert hands, yet enjoys most of its popularity among the lower ranks of tournament players, where it can lead to some strange contracts.

If you ask a self-styled Sharples player to describe his convention, he will quite often say that both 2♣ and 2♢ show major two-suiters with tolerance for the bid minor and hence a virtually guaranteed shortage in the other. This in fact is *Ripstra*, the main difference being that a Sharples 2♣ does not guarantee 4 cards in hearts, while a Ripstra one does. Ripstra is an unsatisfactory defence because of its low frequency; players who use it, under whatever name, tend to introduce it on unsuitable shapes, with predictable results.

Cansino is a hybrid type which uses 2♣ to show a hand playable in three suits including clubs, while 2♢ is bid on major two-suiters. Again, the frequency of occurrence is rather too low. When the inventor, Jonathan Cansino, was playing with Jeremy Flint in the European Championships, the pair were frequently asked to outline the theoretical advantages of the convention. Cansino feigned a haughty indifference, but his partner was more forthcoming, modestly admitting to the need for a self-inflicted handicap!

Other defences are occasionally encountered, but those described above are the best known. We favour the two-suited type, of which Aspro seems the best; this convention steers an acceptable middle path between the rather misty Sharples approach and the over-precise Ripstra or Cansino.

A useful addition to the armoury is an agreement to play a double of 1NT by a passed hand, or a double of a strong 1NT in any position, as showing a major or minor two-suiter. (If your defence includes another bid for a major two-suiter, then such a double always shows the minors). The penalty double of a strong 1NT – which, incidentally, should include the wide-range Blue Club 1NT – is very unlikely to be a rewarding exercise, and the loss of this option is no loss at all. The responder to the double bids his better minor, and the doubler now bids 2♡ if he has both majors.

Finally, it should be noted that a 2NT overcall of 1NT should always be used to show a powerful two-suiter, too distributional for a penalty double and too strong for a conventional overcall. To bid, say, an Aspro 2♣ on:

♠6   ♡AKJ97   ♢AQJ853   ♣10

is to submit the convention to a strain for which it was not designed, and will lead to a comical result when partner holds, say:

♠J653   ♡Q2   ♢K   ♣986532

when you will not enjoy being defeated in 2♣ with eleven tricks cold in either red suit.

E.   DEFENCE TO ARTIFICIAL 1♣ OPENINGS

With the increasing popularity of 1♣ systems in the tournament world, much mental energy has been expended on trying to make life difficult for the 1♣ bidder and his partner. Some of the enthusiasts who have adopted Precision, for instance, devote enormous amounts of loving effort to developing their constructive sequences after a 1♣ opening, but tend to become disorganised and accident-prone in the face of energetic sabotage. Playing on this weakness can produce gratifying results. It is standard practice, and unquestionably effective, to follow a basic policy of passing on strong hands and overcalling on weak ones; this is undoubtedly where the weak jump overcall comes into its own.

It is generally accepted that natural overcalls on weakish hands with a suit not good enough to risk a jump are unlikely to be successful. You will not greatly inconvenience opponents unless partner has a good enough fit to raise a barrage, and if they do find their best contract you will certainly have helped them play it. It is more practical to play a scheme of two-suited overcalls, doubling the chances that partner will have a fitting suit in which to raise the ante. The most popular such defence is *Truscott*, in which a simple suit overcall shows the suit bid and the next suit above that – thus 1♠, for instance, shows spades and clubs. A double of the artificial bid shows that suit and the non-touching one (in the case of 1♣, then, the double shows clubs and hearts), while 1NT shows the remaining pair (spades and diamonds in this instance). The same defence can be used by the player sitting under the 1♣ bidder after a conventional response on his right: thus after a Blue Club 1♣ opening and an artificial 1♠ response, double shows spades and diamonds, 1NT clubs and hearts. Like most two-suited conventions this one is effective only if restricted to genuine two-suited hands, so that your partner will feel free to bid to the limit if he has a good fit.

Some exotic defences to the strong 1♣ have been devised. In the 1972 Olympiad Jeremy Flint used a method whereby a non-vulnerable jump overcall might be a normal 6-card suit, might be 6 cards in the suit *above* the one bid, or might be 4-4-4-1 with the shortage in the suit bid! Not surprisingly this produced some curious results, notably on this hand:

North-South Game, Dealer North

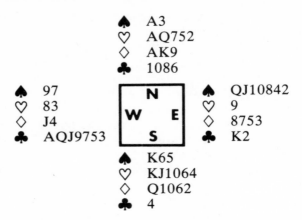

The bidding was unusual: North opened an artificial 1♣, and East overcalled with the ambiguous jump overcall of 2♡. South, playing Sputnik doubles, could only pass, which he did at normal tempo as an ethical player should. West passed . . . and so did North, who had forgotten his partner was playing Sputnik and decided to accept a plus score. 'Plus 1430,' said East-West's team-mates at the scoring-up time. 'Minus 350,' was the reply.

6. Protection

In the average player's vocabulary, protection by the fourth hand after an opening bid has been passed round is rich in misunderstanding. A take-out double in the protective position should follow all the rules for immediate doubles, except that the strength can be up to one full trick weaker. The logic behind this is that your partner may have a good hand on which he had no convenient bid available – for instance, if the opening bid was 1♠ it would have been correct to pass on any of the following hands:

(a)	♠J75	(b)	♠KJ865	(c)	♠KJ97
	♡AK		♡Q		♡A8
	◇A8642		◇AK74		◇K74
	♣J83		♣J83		♣QJ83

Hand (a) with its sketchy diamond suit and good defensive strength does not justify a 2-level overcall. Hand (b) demonstrates the sound general rule that with 5 cards in opponents' suit it is virtually never right to bid. Hand (c) is almost good enough for a 1NT overcall, but not quite, and no other bid even comes into consideration.

When you are in the protective position it is your duty to allow for partner's having been obliged to pass on a hand as good as these, and so you must be prepared to 'protect' his pass on slender values. Since one of the opponents has now admitted to extreme weakness, it is less dangerous for you to enter the fray than it would have been for your partner to do so on one of the hands shown above. Below are three examples of hands which should re-open with a double of an opening 1♠:

(a) ♠A3   (b) ♠3   (c) ♠A
    ♡J10742   ♡J1074   ♡1074
    ◇QJ5   ◇Q1053   ◇QJ1053
    ♣K92   ♣AQ92   ♣K942

A useful yardstick when deciding whether to protect with a double is mentally to add an extra ace to your hand: if this would justify a take-out double in the immediate position, a protective double would now be correct.

The ultra-light protective double can strike gold when partner has made a trap pass. This deal was the subject of much indignation when it occurred in a club pairs event a few years ago:

Dealer North, N-S Game

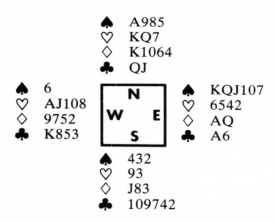

```
              ♠  A985
              ♡  KQ7
              ◇  K1064
              ♣  QJ

♠ 6             N            ♠  KQJ107
♡ AJ108                      ♡  6542
◇ 9752       W     E         ◇  AQ
♣ K853          S            ♣  A6

              ♠  432
              ♡  93
              ◇  J83
              ♣  109742
```

North might have been wise to down-value his club holding and open a weak 1NT but in practice 1♠ was a popular choice. Some Easts could not resist finding a bid, which usually led to a contract of 4♡ or 3NT, both of which are unbeatable. The Easts who correctly passed were mostly let down by their partners, only one West finding the re-opening double – though very thin, the double is certainly correct, as you can see by adding the ◇A to the hand, which would now justify an immediate take-out double because of the 4-card heart suit. 1♠ doubled became the final contract, and East-West collected 1400. The interesting thing was that several East-West pairs asked *West* how she had known she should pass her partner's double, and even suggested that the double must have been made in thunderous tones! The idea that West herself might have doubled ('on only eight points') simply did not occur to them.

When you are in the protective position you know that both your opponents are limited, one by his failure to open with a 2-bid and the other by his pass. You may therefore enter the auction with much less fear of conceding a penalty than in other positions. So all bids may be made on reduced values, though in other respects they conform to normal requirements: an over-call shows a good suit, a jump overcall a good 6-card suit, and a double tolerance for all the unbid suits or a stronger hand unsuitable for other action. The protective 1NT overcall is slightly different, however, as it does not necessarily promise a guard in the opponents' suit. This overcall traditionally showed 11-14 points and a balanced hand, but this arrangement does cause difficulties in the bidding of stronger balanced hands. Two alternative solutions to this problem are in current use, and we would strongly advise you to adopt one of these in a regular partnership.

One method involves the use of an 11-16 point protective 1NT, with a Crowhurst-type 2♣ inquiry available to responder. Over 2♣, the 1NT bidder rebids 2NT with 15-16; otherwise he treats the bid as Stayman and responds accordingly. This arrangement works very well: it occasionally leads to a frail-looking 2NT with 11 points facing 10, but in practice the information available from opponents' bidding will usually compensate declarer for the lack of high cards.

Jeremy Flint and Terence Reese have evolved a compre-hensive scheme for bidding balanced hands in the protective position. Holding such a hand after one of a suit has been passed round to you, re-open as follows:

11-14   1NT
15-17   2♣
18-19   Double, then bid no trumps
20-21   2NT
22+   Double, then jump in no trumps

All these bids except 1NT guarantee cover in the enemy suit. Over the ambiguous 2♣, responder can inquire by bidding the enemy suit – now 2NT shows the balanced 15-17, and any other bid is natural and shows a normal protective club overcall. (If the enemy suit is clubs, of course, no inquiry is necessary!) The loss of the Unusual 2NT overcall is unimportant, as such hands can be introduced in other ways now that there is no need for pre-emptive effect.

The principles of protection also apply in cases where the opponents have made more than one bid. Here however aggression needs to be tempered with a certain amount of discretion. If they have stopped at a low level despite not finding a satisfactory fit, this cannot necessarily be interpreted as a sign of weakness. When they have an apparent misfit it is often more prudent to leave them to dangle rather than take protective action which may let them off the hook. However, it is not wrong for an aggressive player to make a protective double in such a situation – this is the safest form of action, as partner may be able to convert the double to a penalty one. In an earlier chapter we considered this sequence:

1♣	No	1♡	No
2♣	No	No	Dbl

and made the point that the doubler should be well provided for in the heart department; he hopes his partner can pass for penalties, but is prepared for a withdrawal to one of the unbid suits. This is unlikely to lead to a bad result, whereas an overcall in the same situation could be very dangerous. Similarly:

1♣	No	1♠	No
2♣	No	2♠	No
No	?		

This should be left well alone unless your hand is particularly suited to doubling. Opponents could have as much as 24 or 25 points, and have wisely stopped because of the bad fit. Consider these hands in the light of that bidding:

(a)	(b)	(c)
♠AJ92	♠Q5	♠J
♡KJ86	♡KJ632	♡KJ105
◇Q1062	◇KJ72	◇A1095
♣2	♣J8	♣K983

With (a) you might have chanced a shaded double on the first round, but it is too late now – sitting under the enemy spade suit your hand has limited prospects in attack, and you should pass smoothly and be well satisfied if you beat the contract. With hand (b) you have better support for the unbid suits, but your defensive values are non-existent, and you will have a nasty moment if you double protectively and hear partner pass for penalties. Hand (c) is the one on which to chance a double: though this may result in the occasional self-inflicted wound, it is more likely to bring in a rewarding 500 penalty. The difference here, of course, is that you are sitting over the enemy clubs, and hope that partner will be similarly placed over the spade bidder.

If opponents have stopped at a low level despite finding a fit, you can safely be more enterprising, as it is likely that your side too can find a place to play.

	(a)		(b)		(c)
	♠ K1064		♠ AJ6		♠ K764
	♡ 75		♡ 7		♡ A75
	◇ KQ5		◇ KQ852		◇ AJ5
	♣ Q953		♣ J1053		♣ 953

After the bidding has gone 1♡ on your right, No Bid from you, 2♡ on your left passed back to you, you should certainly enter the lists with a double on hands (a) and (b). With hand (c) it is safer to pass, as any other action may result in exchanging a small plus for a small minus. At duplicate pairs, however, you could chance your arm and bid, as at this form of the game you must take more risks in your attempts to win the part-score battle – the sound maxim here is not to let your opponents play undoubled at the level of one or two unless they appear to have a misfit, or strike you as capable of grossly undervaluing their cards!

The other big danger faced by the would-be protector is that inept opponents have indeed undervalued their joint holding, and given a second chance may find their game after all. Every player has occasionally been made to look foolish in this position. You must stoically accept that this will happen to you from time to time, for the rewards from a well judged protective bid will outweigh the occasional embarrassing disaster. However, it is essential to measure the possible profit against the possible loss. Remember that your partner failed to take any action in the immediate position – this may sometimes give you a clue as to whether the hand really belongs to your side or to the enemy.

The comparative rank of your suits and your opponents' can be a decisive factor. Often you may protect in the hope of stealing a part-score because you know you can outbid your opponents at the two-level. For the same reason you might pass an apparently similar hand because you suspect opponents have the spade fit. With this hand, for instance:

♠763 ♡KJ1052 ◇8 ♣KQ86

after an opening 1 ◇ on your right has been raised to 2 ◇, passed back to you, you should go quietly; it is too likely that if you bid 2 ♡ now right-hand opponent will re-open with 2 ♠ 'on the way' to 3 ◇, and will play there in a 4-3 fit for a good score. But if you transpose the heart and spade holdings, a protective 2 ♠ overcall is well worth while.

Protection After Passing
To amplify the general instruction we have given on the subject of protection, we must consider the extra definition that arises when the protector has passed. Clearly, unless he has overlooked an ace, his strength will be limited to 12 points; thus he is free to use a variety of calls not otherwise available. In each case we will suppose that you passed as dealer, and a 1 ◇ opening on your left has come back to you. Here are some hands you might hold:

(a) ♠KJ1096 ♡KJ1094 ◇– ♣J32

The best bid here is 2 ◇, obviously requiring partner to choose his better major. The snag about a double is the distinct possibility that 1 ◇ doubled will become the final contract, where your lack of defensive tricks and trump void will give you a hard time in defence. Note that this hand conforms to our earlier suggestion that you should use Michaels cue-bids after passing, though in this case no specific agreement is necessary.

(b) ♠KJ109 ♡KQ42 ◇J ♣J1094

Here a double is in order – if partner passes you will relish the outcome.

(c) ♠KJ109864 ♡J1098 ◇3 ♣A

You displayed considerable restraint in not opening this one. Clearly you must re-open now, and the best bid is 3♠ – there is considerable danger that East-West have a club fit, and this pre-emptive effort should make it hard for them to find it. Incidentally, a first-class partner will appreciate the reason for your strange antics in the bidding, and deduce that you could not open with a pre-empt on the first round because of your strength in the other major.

(d) ♠KJ64 ♡Q1096 ◇KJ3 ♣42

This one is a minimum protective 1NT. Note that your holding in the majors makes it less probable that opponents have a fit in either of them.

(e) ♠AQJ1043 ♡Q1063 ◇64 ♣2

Here a jump overcall of 2♠ is in order. You might or might not be able to buy the contract in 1♠, but 2♠ has more pre-emptive value, and also describes your hand better should your partner be strong.

(f) ♠73 ♡Q32 ◇AKJ4 ♣J532

This is the time to pass. Note the difference between this hand and (d) above: here it is highly likely that your opponents have a better fit in spades than in diamonds, while your partner's pass was clearly not based on strength in the diamond suit. It is virtually certain that the enemy will outbid you in the majors if you give them the chance; they may even make game.

There is a further general point to be made in connection with protecting after a pass. What was the opening bid? If it was a minor suit, partner will seldom have been inconvenienced by it – in the modern game he can even overcall with a fair 4-card suit. You should assume that he would bid freely over a minor-suit opening if he had anything to bid, and you should therefore protect more vigorously if it was a major that was opened. An extension to this arises in the Italian style of varying the strength of a protective 1NT depending on the opening bid: they require considerably more for 1NT over 1♣ than for 1NT over 1♠. As we see it this is a very logical treatment.

The Protector's Partner

So far we have examined only the problems of the player who is protecting. His partner too must adapt his bidding to the special circumstances. Suppose that an opening 1♢ on your right has been passed round to your partner, who has protected with a double. What do you bid on each of the following hands:

(a) ♠KJ43   (b) ♠KJ4   (c) ♠KQ4
    ♡Q2   ♡Q2   ♡Q42
    ♢A8764   ♢AJ43   ♢AQ64
    ♣A4   ♣10762   ♣J42

(d) ♠AQ43   (e) ♠A7643   (f) ♠AQ104
    ♡KJ52   ♡A8642   ♡6
    ♢J42   ♢42   ♢AQ1098
    ♣73   ♣3   ♣K76

On hand (a) the best bid is 2♢. If you would have passed for penalties, do not be surprised if you run out of amiable partners. Nothing is worse for partnership confidence than a penalty pass of a take-out double which misfires. The doubler probably has a weak, shapely hand and is made to feel he has been over-bold. But the real villain is the player who passes when he lacks sufficient intermediates in the trump suit to be able to control the defence. So here we bid 2♢, the most flexible bid: 4♠ will probably be the best contract, but if partner has only 3 spades 3NT could well be the answer. It would be a bad error to introduce no trumps yourself without investigating the spade fit.

On hand (b) you should bid 1NT. Yes, only one – 2NT would be a gross overstatement. Remember that your partner can be quite weak for his protective double.

By the same token, with hand (c) 2NT is enough. A few extra 10s and 9s would justify a borderline 3NT.

Hand (d) may look quite promising, but we consider 1♡ enough for the moment. We are opposed to what we call the 'Baby Kangaroo System', characterized by a series of little jumps each time the player has an extra Jack. Our preference is for the doubler to give his partner another chance, except when he is dead minimum for the original double.

Hand (e) is a very different matter. With your excellent shape and controls there should be a play for game even opposite minimum values. The best bid to start investigations here is 2 ◊.

As for hand (f), the solution here depends on the vulnerability and the method of scoring. If opponents are vulnerable it would be a superfluous act of mercy to bid again and save them from their fate – pass and take the money. At adverse vulnerability, however, it would be wrong to pass; it is always hard work getting the 700 we need to compensate us for missing a vulnerable game. Start with 2 ◊, and if no spade fit appears settle for 3NT.

7. The Sputnik double

The double is by far the most flexible weapon available to a pair who wish to extend their partnership understanding and sharpen the accuracy of their bidding methods. The theory of conventions in bidding states that a convention is efficient if the profit anticipated from its use will outweigh the loss sustained by the inability to use the bid in its natural sense. Since this has to be calculated in conjunction with frequency of occurrence, it is not always easy to decide whether a convention will pay its way or not. Nevertheless, most good tournament pairs accept that it is sound to find alternative uses for many low-level doubles which – in their natural sense – would be for penalties. Not that the penalties are to be lightly scorned, but their frequency is low, and the conventional use gives sufficient advantage to outweigh the loss, particularly since (as we shall see) it may still be possible to obtain the penalty in another way. We have already examined one of these low-level conventional doubles, the Responsive Double. In this chapter we look at the most radical of them all, one of the most interesting and valuable developments in modern bidding – the negative or Sputnik double.

The term 'Sputnik' was coined by the famous American partnership of Alvin Roth and Tobias Stone for their version of the 'negative double'; the only reason for the name was that the convention dated from the same period as the Russian satellite Sputnik I. The situation for which the convention was originally designed was this:

♠653 ♡KQ105 ◇AJ104 ♣52

After 1♣ from your partner and a 1♠ overcall on your right, this hand presents a problem on natural methods, where a forcing 2 ◊ response takes the bidding too high too fast. This is a perfect Sputnik hand: you double, showing the two unbid suits with a single bid.

The effects of borrowing a bid in this way have to be carefully studied to ensure that a new unbiddable hand has not been created. What about this hand? say the 'naturalists':

♠KJ10964   ♡A75   ◊642   ♣7

Not only have you lost the opportunity to punish the reckless overcall with a crushing penalty, but you have left yourself with an unbiddable hand. The only possible candidate is a natural 2♠, but that is far too valuable in its normal artificial sense. The answer is that most experts who use Sputnik doubles resort to compulsory protection by the opener in situations where his partner may hold a penalty double and have been forced to pass:

South	West	North	East
1♡	1♠	No	No

As South after the bidding shown you hold a hand of this type:

(a) ♠6	(b) ♠A7
♡KQ863	♡KQ74
◊AQ74	◊KQ64
♣Q74	♣874

– that is, a minimum opening bid with no great shape or playing strength. If not playing Sputnik, you should not reopen on either hand. Using the convention, you must adopt a rather different viewpoint. Ask yourself first whether it is at all likely that your partner has a penalty-double type of hand. If it is, you must bid. Ask yourself also whether, if he had made a penalty double, you would have stood it. If so, your re-opening bid should be a double . . . and double is the right bid now on both the hands shown above. Contrast these two:

(c) ♠KJ62	(d) ♠75
♡AQ1063	♡KQJ976
◊Q74	◊KJ54
♣7	♣Q

With hand (c) you cannot reasonably expect partner to have enough spades to warrant a sound penalty double, and you can pass. With (d), you cannot by any means rule out the possibility that your partner is well endowed with spades, and you should therefore re-open, as he may be quite strong. However, you would not have passed his penalty double, so you cannot double now – bid 2 ◇.

This method appears to leave the door open for guileful opponents to intervene psychically. We still believe that, even without prepared defence to psychics, you are more likely to gain than lose against opponents who resort to these tactics, as long as you keep your head. A greater danger is that you might reach the 2- or 3-level with grossly inadequate values, or you may allow your 'forcing' pass to enhance the bidding machinery of resourceful opponents. This is an example from a pairs tournament:

Dealer West, Love All

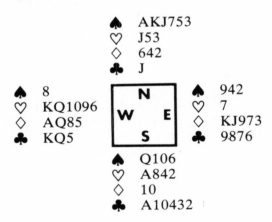

```
                    ♠  AKJ753
                    ♡  J53
                    ◇  642
                    ♣  J
        ♠  8          N          ♠  942
        ♡  KQ1096              ♡  7
        ◇  AQ85    W     E      ◇  KJ973
        ♣  KQ5       S          ♣  9876
                    ♠  Q106
                    ♡  A842
                    ◇  10
                    ♣  A10432
```

This was the bidding:

South	West	North	East
	1♡	1♠	No
No!	Dbl	No	2◇
3◇	No	4♠	No
No	No		

South knew from the strength of his spade holding that West was virtually forced to reopen, and profited from this chance to show his singleton diamond, allowing North to appreciate the power of the fit.

The danger exemplified by this hand may be reduced if you appreciate that although protection on mimimum hands is normal procedure, you will occasionally take a chance and pass when your judgement suggests that there is more danger of climbing too high than there is of missing a game. For example, you hold the following hand, with your side only vulnerable:

♠6 ♡KQ53 ◇K53 ♣A10742

You open 1♣, and a 1♠ overcall on your left is passed back to you. Now it is safer to pass. Take these two possible hands for your partner:

(a)	♠Q105	(b)	♠KJ10975
	♡1074		♡A7
	◇J862		◇7
	♣Q63		♣K865

If you double and find partner with hand (b) you will make a handsome profit; but realism insists that he is more likely to have hand (a), when alert opponents may extract a painful penalty from 2♣ doubled. However, many leading experts now play that this situation is forcing, unless the opener has reason to be *sure* that his partner is not trapping. Such reason could be that he himself is long in the enemy suit, or perhaps a display of interest by his right-hand opponent. With:

♠K73 ♡KQ84 ◇6 ♣AQ953

it would obviously be sound to pass.

Since the early days of Sputnik, experts have modified its use until there are three variations of the convention encountered in tournament play.

A. LIMITED USE

Many players limit the Sputnik double to those cases where the pre-emptive effect of the overcall is most felt. The commonest such restricted use occurs after an opening bid of 1♣ or 1◇ and an overcall of 1♠. A double now shows 8-11 points with 4 or more cards in hearts, and either support for partner's suit or 4 cards in the unbid minor. After 1♣ from partner, 1♠ on your right, any of these hands would qualify for a double under this version of the convention:

	(a)		(b)		(c)
	♠653		♠5		♠A6
	♡KQ105		♡Q8643		♡AK85
	◇AJ104		◇643		◇10753
	♣52		♣AQ75		♣943

Doubles of other overcalls, or at a higher level, can retain their penalty meaning with this interpretation of Sputnik.

Rebids by opener are natural, based on the assumption that responder has 'bid' both unbid suits. Opener can rebid his own suit, call no trumps with an adequate spade holding, or 'support' one of the responder's suits. This support is limited, and may on occasions be made with a 3-card holding if no other bid is available. Holding:

♠542 ♡AQ6 ◇AK763 ♣J4

after 1◇ from you, 1♠ overcall, Double from partner, the best bid is 2♡, just as it would have been had partner been able to respond 1♡ to the opening bid.

The Sputnik double is not completely forcing, but the opener should only pass with an exceptionally good defensive hand and sequential spades. With this:

♠QJ109 ♡K6 ◇AK64 ♣A75

after the same bidding (1◇-1♠-Dbl-No) you might risk a pass.

An alternative restricted use which has recently gained some adherents is to play all doubles of 1- and 2-level overcalls as Sputnik if a major suit has been cut out, the double promising the excluded major or majors. Thus 1♡-2♣-Dbl is Sputnik and shows spades, but 1♠-2◇-Dbl is for penalties as usual. This method is open to an obvious theoretical objection: the more majors an overcall cuts out, the more attractive it is and the more risks the overcaller will take . . . so the times when you are most likely to need a penalty double are the times when you are least likely to have it! This method seems to offer no advantages over the 'general use', described below.

B. GENERAL USE

Another method of playing the Sputnik double is for any double of an overcall at the 1- or 2-level to be for take-out, showing values in both unbid suits. The theory is similar to the restricted use, but there are some additional negative inferences. For example, if the bidding has started 1♣-1♡-1♠, the 1♠ bidder presumably has either a 5-card suit or a hand outside the point range for a double. This can be very useful, allowing the opener to support freely to the 2-level on as little as 3 small spades. The opener can pass for penalties more freely when the overcall is made at the 2-level.

Even pre-emptive jump overcalls can be included in the Sputnik scheme, but the lack of precision when the auction reaches these high levels means that there can no longer be strict requirements for the double. It merely shows useful values, and the opener may well pass for penalties even with no particular trump strength.

C. TWO-WAY SPUTNIK

The most modern and expert use of the Sputnik double is as a two-way weapon. Sputnik doubles apply after all simple and jump overcalls, and show one of two types of hand. The first type contains support for the unbid suits, and about 8-11 points: this is known as 'Low-Power Sputnik' and is similar to the types described above. The lower limit for the point-count is flexible, and fewer than 8 points would be acceptable in some cases. After 1♣-1♢, it would not be unreasonable to double on:

♠Q1085 ♡KJ106 ♢54 ♣1063

especially at match-point duplicate. This avoids a not uncommon problem when partner holds:

♠K973 ♡Q82 ♢73 ♣AKJ8

If you reply 1♡ and next hand raises to 2♢ (or worse still 3♢) the spade fit may be lost for ever. If you have doubled to suggest both majors, partner can 'raise' spades freely at his second turn.

The lower limit should also be raised when the double would

force a 3-level bid from partner, as after the bidding 1♣-2♠-Dbl. It would not be safe to double here on:

♠643 ♡KQ64 ◇K753 ♣83

which would have been a good minimum double of 1♠.

The second type of hand is shown by following the double with a change of suit. This is known as 'High-Power Sputnik', and is used to initiate a forcing sequence. The object of this idea is to cater for the otherwise unbiddable hand of this type:

♠KQJ1064 ♡63 ◇972 ♣95

After 1♡ from partner, 2♣ on your right, you want to bid 2♠ . . . but you want to add in parentheses ('non-forcing'). Using two-way Sputnik, this is exactly what you are able to do. A change of suit when the intervention has raised the level of the response is non-forcing and defensive. Note that in the sequence shown a response of 2◇ would be forcing, as the same bid could have been made without the intervention.

These three hands would all start with a high-power double after the bidding has begun 1♡-2♣:

	(a) ♠KQ753	(b) ♠KQ95	(c) ♠A4
	♡A6	♡7	♡KJ753
	◇KQ7	◇AK742	◇AK64
	♣753	♣K53	♣84

On hand (a) you will bid the spade suit on the next round over a rebid from partner of, say, 2◇. This shows a strong hand and a 5-card suit. If partner 'supports' your spades at once by bidding 2♠ over the double, you can force again with 3♣ (the opponents' suit), and then bid spades strongly on the following round.

With hand (b) you intend to bid diamonds next time, which will be forcing. The advantage of doubling now rather than bidding a forcing 2◇ is that partner may be able to show spade support immediately. If you bid 2◇ and next hand bids 3♣, partner with:

♠A1084 ♡AJ853 ◇Q6 ♣J5

will not be able to move, and though you can mention the spades at your next turn the situation will have become rather unclear, and partner will not be sure that you really have a 4-card spade suit.

On hand (c) you propose to jump in hearts next time, showing powerful support and slam ambition: the hand is too good for a delayed game raise via 2 ◊, while an immediate force in diamonds would suggest a better suit.

Hand (a) above was well bid when it occurred in team-of-four play:

Dealer East, E-W Game

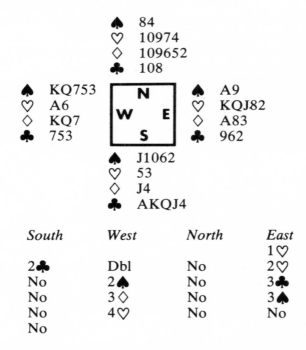

	♠	84	
	♡	10974	
	◊	109652	
	♣	108	

♠ KQ753		♠ A9
♡ A6	**N**	♡ KQJ82
◊ KQ7	**W E**	◊ A83
♣ 753	**S**	♣ 962

♠	J1062	
♡	53	
◊	J4	
♣	AKQJ4	

South	West	North	East
			1♡
2♣	Dbl	No	2♡
No	2♠	No	3♣
No	3◊	No	3♠
No	4♡	No	No
No			

Note that it is not easy to reach the only makable game even without intervention. In the auction given, East's 3♣ shows yet another use of the versatile cue-bid of the enemy suit: no club guard (or he would bid 2NT), nothing very much in diamonds (or he bids 3 ◊), not 6 cards in hearts or 3 in spades. West's 3 ◊ showed values in the suit, enabling East to know he could commit the side to game with his 3♠ bid, and after both partners have shown their modest support for each other's long suits they are able to settle in the more solid of the two.

It must be pointed out that if two-way Sputnik is being played it becomes very dangerous for the opener to make a penalty pass, as the doubler may have a very strong hand with little suitability for defence. Because of this factor, there is something to be said for not using high-power Sputnik on hands containing good support for partner's suit, such as hand (c) above. This will allow opener to make the occasional penalty pass:

♠KJ1082 ♡4 ◇AK1065 ♣94

After 1♠ from you, 2◇ on your left, double from partner it is safe to pass if you are sure that partner is not lurking with massive spade support. Without this understanding, it is better to play the double as 100% forcing.

Apart from this, there are no specific distributional requirements for a high-power Sputnik double. It may help to clarify the general instruction given above, however, if we describe the requirements for the low-power double in more detail. As we like to interpret the convention, the message of the double is as follows:

(i) If the opener has bid a minor and the suit doubled is a major, the double promises 4 cards in the other major. If the overcall was 1♠ the doubler may have 5 hearts.

(ii) If the opener and the overcaller have both bid minors, the double shows at least one 4-card major, and at least reasonable support for the other.

(iii) 1♡-1♠-Dbl promises something in both minors, as otherwise there must be an alternative bid available.

(iv) 1♠-2♡-Dbl shows nothing more than values to compete at the 3-level, with no more convenient bid available.

There may well be length in both minors, but it is clearly necessary to be able to double on some such hand as:

♠Q52 ♡942 ◇AKJ8 ♣Q103

where any alternative bid is quickly seen to be out of the question.

As for the non-forcing free bid in a new suit, this applies

whenever the suit you are bidding has been excluded by the overcall. Free bids in non-excluded suits are forcing in the normal way.

D.   SPUTNIK IN ARTIFICIAL SYSTEMS

The dangers of pre-emptive action against an artificial system make the frequent use of Sputnik doubles essential. In Precision, it is standard to play Sputnik doubles of all simple and jump overcalls of an artificial 1♣ opening. In Blue Club, doubles of simple overcalls have a conventional meaning, but the Sputnik interpretation is recommended at higher levels. Since no suits are shown by the double, the overcall is ignored as far as possible, and further bidding by either partner is natural, including bids in opponents' suit. This serves as an automatic safety device against psychic intervention, a popular pastime against artificial systems. Here is a hand where one of the authors was able to deal efficiently with a psychic overcall:

Dealer West, E-W game

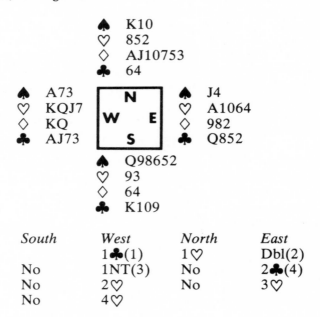

```
                  ♠  K10
                  ♡  852
                  ◇  AJ10753
                  ♣  64

    ♠  A73        N        ♠  J4
    ♡  KQJ7                ♡  A1064
    ◇  KQ      W     E     ◇  982
    ♣  AJ73       S        ♣  Q852

                  ♠  Q98652
                  ♡  93
                  ◇  64
                  ♣  K109
```

South	West	North	East
	1♣(1)	1♡	Dbl(2)
No	1NT(3)	No	2♣(4)
No	2♡	No	3♡
No	4♡		

(1) 17+ points
(2) Sputnik, 4-7 points
(3) 17-19, balanced
(4) Stayman

One of the authors, long wedded to Blue Club, has found a variation on the Sputnik idea to be very valuable in practice. Because of the popularity of very weak jump overcalls after the artificial 1♣, it is useful to have a penalty double available to punish opponents when they go too far. A simple solution is to use a 2NT response over a weak jump as Sputnik, showing the values for a positive response without any particular strong suit to bid. The same method could of course be used with other artificial systems.

E. 'OPENER'S SPUTNIK'

This final variation on the Sputnik theme is a new idea which has been tried out in one tournament partnership by one of the authors, and has proved completely effective. It applies in a situation we have already examined in Chapter 2: you open one of a suit, next hand passes, partner changes the suit, and right-hand opponent overcalls in a third suit. We recommended earlier that a pass in this position should be played as forcing, and that in standard methods a double is for penalties. We can now suggest a more efficient scheme for those who are attracted by the Sputnik principle.

The sort of hand that causes problems is this:

♠KJ98 ♡6 ◇AQJ54 ♣K83

You open 1◇, partner replies 1♡, and next hand intervenes with 2♣. In standard methods you can do no more than bid 2◇, which may lead to a silly result when next hand raises to 3♣ and your partner holds:

♠Q1052 ♡A98532 ◇K ♣54

Clearly he can hardly bid 3♠ now, and nor can you when the bidding comes back to you. Yet 4♠ is an excellent contract, so if you can never bid the suit at all there must be something wrong with existing methods. It is clearly dangerous to reduce the requirements for a reverse of 2♠ on the second round, a move which would anyway leave you with a problem when you really have reversing values.

The answer is to play a double by the opener in such sequences as showing 4 cards in the unbid suit without values for a reverse. With the hands shown above, bidding 4♠ is now child's play: you double the 2♣ overcall, and whether next hand raises or not it is easy enough for your partner to jump straight to 4♠.

It is always agreeable to be able to cope efficiently with opponents' intervention, but it is much more so to be able to use that intervention to show a feature of your hand that could not otherwise have been shown. In a congress pairs event, one of the authors held:

♠65   ♡AJ83   ◇AQJ76   ♣94

and opened 1◇. Partner bid 2♣, and opener would normally have to rebid 2◇, but right-hand opponent came to the rescue with a 2♠ overcall. Opener doubled to show his hearts, next hand passed, and responder with:

♠Q73   ♡K1072   ◇4   ♣AQ632

bid 3♡, which became the final contract and was just made. At other tables opener had had to pass the overcall, and when this came round to the 2♣ bidder he was fixed: those who recklessly bid 3♡ were raised to 4♡ and went down; those who doubled collected +100 at best and —470 at worst; the no-trumpers got what they deserved, as did the no-bidders. The only other heart part-scores were collected by pairs who responded 1♡ on the first round – well, even mongrels have their moments.

It is a matter of taste whether the method outlined above should be extended to situations where it is not strictly necessary. For instance:

South	West	North	East
South	*West*	*North*	*East*
1◇	No	1♡	1♠

Here South has not been robbed of any rebid; if he has clubs he can still bid them at the minimum level. However, the reader may feel it is useful to be able to distinguish at once between the following three hands:

(a) ♠Q96   (b) ♠K96   (c) ♠A96
    ♡7   ♡7   ♡7
    ◇AK853   ◇AK853   ◇AKQ53
    ♣QJ74   ♣AQJ4   ♣AQJ4

With no intervention, (a) and (b) both have to bid 2♣, only (c) being worth the full-blooded game force of 3♣. Playing Opener's Sputnik, hand (a) doubles, (b) bids 2♣ and (c) still bids 3♣. The distinction between (a) and (b) may well be very valuable to responder if the spades are raised pre-emptively. For memory reasons, too, it is simplest to use the conventional double in all cases.

And suppose you hold this hand:

♠KJ87 ♡6 ◇AQ982 ♣A74

You open 1◇, partner bids 1♡, and next hand chips in with 1♠. Do you wish you had never heard of Opener's Sputnik? Certainly not. All you do is make your forcing pass, and rely on partner to re-open with a double if he would have stood a penalty double of 1♠ – the usual Sputnik principle, in fact. It was remarked earlier in this book that a penalty pass is often a more effective weapon than a penalty double. This final deal from match-play illustrates why.

Dealer South, Game All

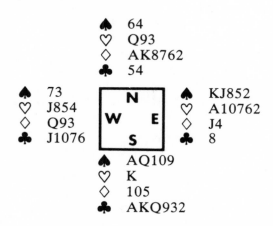

```
              ♠  64
              ♡  Q93
              ◇  AK8762
              ♣  54
♠ 73                        ♠ KJ852
♡ J854      N               ♡ A10762
◇ Q93    W     E            ◇ J4
♣ J1076     S               ♣ 8
              ♠  AQ109
              ♡  K
              ◇  105
              ♣  AKQ932
```

S	W	N	E
1♣	No	1◇	1♠
No(1)	No	Dbl(2)	No
No	No		

(1) Forcing
(2) With two defensive tricks, North can safely double

East's overcall was dangerous at the vulnerability – a double might have been better, but East would have considered this to show a stronger hand, while an 'Unusual' 1NT would have risked taking the bidding too high. East can hardly be blamed for passing on the second round – one something is cheaper than two something, after all – and poor West was not to know that hearts would play better than spades. In the other room the first round of bidding was the same, but then South doubled for penalties; East escaped to 2♡, and North-South would have done best to defend this, but – as so often happens – they misjudged the position and bid on to 3NT, which should have been made but wasn't.

8. The competitive double

The competitive double is one of the most sophisticated of modern additions to the competitive bidding arsenal, and also one of the most worth while. In fact the name is a general one for various unclassifiable types of double which have sprung up like mushrooms in certain competitive situations. Nowadays there are few cases of low-level doubles being universally treated as for penalties, and the collective name for the alternative use is 'competitive'. It is unnecessary for us to describe all the variations at length, and in this chapter we shall restrict ourselves to those most often employed, and those we consider most valuable.

A. BY THE INTERVENING SIDE

There are four basic situations in which this double may be used by the side which has made an overcall:

(i) Neither side has agreed a suit.
(ii) Opener's side only has agreed a suit.
(iii) Our side only has agreed a suit.
(iv) Both sides have agreed suits.

Neither side has agreed a suit
The typical situation is when the auction has followed this type of course:

South	West	North	East
1♡	1♠	2♣	Dbl

This double of a new suit response after a simple overcall can be used in a conventional sense to cope with hands such as this:

♠Q7 ♡853 ♢AQ1075 ♣K53

You can see the problem that arises in natural methods. You are clearly too strong to pass, but 2♢ would suggest a more one-suited hand, whereas you are not at all averse to partner's rebidding his spades. You really need a bid that shows moderate spade support and a good diamond suit. The competitive double describes exactly that type of hand. Partner may sign off in your suit by bidding 2♢, usually on a 3-card suit but occasionally with a doubleton; if he dislikes your diamonds he can sign off in 2♠, while 2NT and any jump bid are natural. If all else fails he can always resort to a bid of one of the opponents' suits.

Before we accept this type of double as a valuable convention, two other matters must be thought out. First, as usual, we must ask ourselves what we are going to do with the hand that justifies a natural penalty double. For example:

♠7 ♡KQ105 ♢A63 ♣KJ1096

After 1♡-1♠-2♣, you can see that opponents are heading for the rocks. Good – let them get on to them. Just pass, and wait for something better on the next round. The sequence shown is normally played as forcing, so why tip them off about the coming disaster before they are thoroughly impaled?

It is possible that the 2♣ bid may not be forcing – for instance, your opponents may be playing Sputnik, or the 2♣ bidder may already have passed. If they are playing non-forcing free bids as a matter of principle, you have two choices: you can either say good-bye to any kind of penalty by bidding 2NT, or you can agree to play normal penalty doubles in such cases. The latter is probably the wiser course. If the change-of-suit is non-forcing because the bidder has already passed, the decision is closer:

South	West	North	East
No	No	1♠	2♣
2♡	Dbl		

Although South's 2♡ is technically non-forcing following his pass, most pairs will not allow the bidding to die there unless the opening was sub-minimum. It seems best to treat West's double as competitive, with the clear understanding that if 2♡ is passed to him East should almost certainly re-open.

As usual there is another side to this question of penalties: the competitive double will sometimes allow you to hook a fish that would normally have escaped. On this hand from match-play East-West were able to harvest a penalty instead of conceding one:

Dealer South, North-South Game

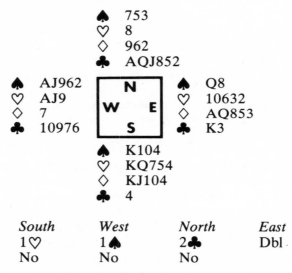

```
              ♠ 753
              ♡ 8
              ♢ 962
              ♣ AQJ852

♠ AJ962        ┌─────────┐      ♠ Q8
♡ AJ9          │   N     │      ♡ 10632
♢ 7            │ W     E │      ♢ AQ853
♣ 10976        │   S     │      ♣ K3
               └─────────┘
              ♠ K104
              ♡ KQ754
              ♢ KJ104
              ♣ 4
```

South	West	North	East
1♡	1♠	2♣	Dbl
No	No	No	

West's hand was ideally suited for a penalty pass of his partner's competitive double, and good defence produced an 800 penalty. Natural bidding is likely to lead East-West to a contract of 2♠, which can be made but may well go down in practice.

Another point to consider is to what level the competitive double should apply. For example, should it be so played after jump responses? For ease of memory as much as anything else we recommend that all such doubles should be played up to the level of 3♡, which allows competition in all part-score zones. If the use is extended to higher levels it may deprive your partner of the option of remaining below the game level. This is not too critical a matter so long as you and your partner are of the same mind.

(ii) Opener's Side Has Agreed a Suit

The typical situation here is when the bidding begins 1♡-1♠-2♡-Dbl. This type of competitive double is similar to the responsive double, described elsewhere. In the modern style, the doubler may have one of two types of hand: either moderate support for spades and at least 4 cards in one of the unbid suits; or tolerance for spades and length in *both* unbid suits. In the sequence given, any of the following hands would qualify for a double:

(a) ♠1075   (b) ♠K7   (c) ♠J7
♡A7   ♡742   ♡74
◇KQ1074   ◇A73   ◇KJ74
♣853   ♣QJ643   ♣AJ643

On hand (a), if partner bids 3♣ you will correct to 3◇, and now he will know he can rely on reasonable spade support. On hand (b) you correct 3◇ to 3♠. Without the double available, you would have a difficult choice to make on all three hands – in each case you are certainly worth a bid, but no obvious bid is available, which is the ideal time to introduce a competitive double.

In our view, this particular type of double should only apply when the doubler's partner will have a choice of bids available at the level of two or three. If the bidding has started 1♡-1♠-3♡-Dbl or 1♠-2♡-3♠-Dbl it is more valuable to play the double as showing a sound raise of partner's suit, not interested in sacrificing against an enemy game, but interested in the possibilities of making a game your way.

An interesting variation on this theme arises when the over-caller's partner has passed, and the overcaller himself reopens with a double. Thus after 1♡ on your right, 1♠ from you, 2♡ on your left passed back to you, what does a double mean? Following the principle established in Chapter 2, we suggest it should show a maximum overcall with only fair spades, prepared to stand a 3-level contract in either minor.

On this hand from rubber bridge, East-West could have benefited from the use of one of these competitive doubles; as it was, they had to toil in a most unsatisfactory spot:

Dealer North, E-W Game

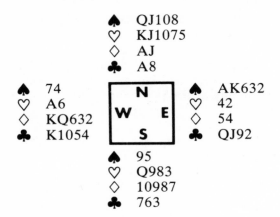

The actual bidding was:

South	West	North	East
		1♡	1♠
2♡	3◇	3♡	No
No	3♠	Dbl	No
No	No		

This contract went one down, declarer losing the obvious five tricks. An expert auction would have been:

South	West	North	East
		1♡	1♠
2♡	Dbl	No	3♣
No	No	3♡	4♣
No	No	No	

It is difficult to construct an intelligent route to the club part-score without the use of a competitive double. If the doubler had held the other type of hand, for instance:

♠Q7 ♡853 ◇KJ1086 ♣A84

he would have converted 3♣ to 3◇, and his partner would now have been able to convert to 3♠ in the confidence of finding a bolster in the trump suit.

At higher levels the doubler must be prepared for preference at the 4-level, and should accordingly be a trick stronger. At the 3-level the overcaller may be inclined to pass for penalties if his hand is defensively suitable. After the bidding has started:

South	West	North	East
1♡	1♠	3♡	Dbl
No	?		

here are three hands which West might hold:

(a) ♠KQ8542	(b) ♠AQ542	(c) ♠AK542
♡74	♡A54	♡J107
◇A84	◇8	◇843
♣76	♣QJ76	♣A6

With hand (a) there is no choice but to bid 3♠, knowing that at least partner will not be altogether threadbare in the suit; with (b) you are worth 4♣; but with (c) a pass is the best chance of a good score: you have three defensive tricks and no sure fit.

This type of aggressive action may shock the staid rubber-bridge player, to whom doubling the opponents into game is the greatest possible sin. We too do not enjoy conceding —470 or —530, but the odd disaster of this kind will be more than compensated for by all the +300s and +500s you collect when your side has the balance of strength but no fit. The full hand in case (c) above may be something like this:

Dealer South, Love All

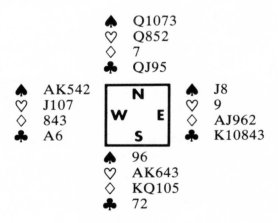

It should be fairly straightforward to collect six tricks in defence with the aid of a trump promotion, but eight tricks is the limit for East-West in a spade contract, while the hand would play very badly in either minor.

(iii) The Defending Side Has Agreed a Suit
The typical situation here is this:

South	West	North	East
1♡	1♠	No	2♠
3♣	Dbl		

or the double may come from East after passes from West and North. It is difficult to construct a type of hand which would have a use for this double in a conventional sense. The only possibility perhaps is to show spades and diamonds, but here the doubler could have conveyed the same message by bidding 3♢ himself. There is a case for using the double here as competitive when the doubler's second suit has been excluded. In the auction shown, if South's second bid had been 3♢ rather than 3♣, a double by West could usefully show clubs.

(iv) Both Sides Have Agreed Suits
Now we assume that the auction has begun:

South	West	North	East
1♡	1♠	2♡	2♠
3♡	Dbl		

or again the double may come from East in the protective position. It is difficult to imagine the penalty double being much use unless opponents are very undisciplined; equally there seems no use whatever for a normal type of competitive double. If West in the sequence shown has mediocre spades and values in both minors, plus the extra strength to compete at this level, surely he makes a normal take-out double on the first round? Similarly, if the double comes from East: why did he not make a competitive double at his first turn? The most sensible use for this type of double seems to us to be to treat it in the same way as one by the *opening* side after both sides have agreed suits: that is, to show a hand which is prepared to compete once more in the agreed suit, but does not want partner to sacrifice at any higher level. In the sequence given, West might hold:

♠AK753 ♡96 ◇AJ5 ♣Q102

He is prepared to go to 3♠, but he would not want his partner to go on to 4♠ over 4♡. This type of double will be discussed more fully in the section on the opening side.

B.   BY THE OPENING SIDE

Again, there are four possible situations, some of them overlapping with ordinary take-out and Sputnik doubles:

(i)   Neither side has agreed a suit
(ii) Opener's side only has agreed a suit
(iii) Intervening side only has agreed a suit
(iv) Both sides have agreed suits

(i) Neither Side Has Agreed a Suit
There are a great many situations that come under this heading, and to classify them we need to go back to the rules governing an ordinary take-out double. For example:

South	West	North	East
1♣	No	1♡	1♠
No	No	Dbl	

Here the doubler's partner has already bid a suit, so this double is in theory for penalties. But in this sequence:

South	West	North	East
1♣	1♡	No	2◇
Dbl			

the double is for take-out, showing the unbid suit, spades, but wanting to preserve the possibility of a penalty if partner has a powerful holding in opponent's suits.

In short, the competitive double as such does not occur when neither side has agreed a suit, and many of these doubling situations have already been discussed in Chapter 2.

(ii) Opener's Side Only Has Agreed a Suit
Here there may be a distinction between cases where the double comes from the player who originally bid the agreed suit, and

those where it is made by his partner. This is because the supporter's assets are clearly limited. Furthermore, if he doubles for penalties the quality of this double is clearly limited by his failure to double on the previous round. In our discussion of co-operative doubles we saw how the responder could safely make a tentative double in this type of sequence:

South	West	North	East
1♡	1♠	2♡	No
No	2♠	Dbl	

If responder wishes to suggest the possibility of an advance, possibly in another strain, he can try the effect of 2NT. Suppose in the auction given he holds:

♠7   ♡Q74   ◇KJ63   ♣QJ742

He has something in hand, but a bid of 3♡ (unless playing a 5-card major system) would be too inflexible. 2NT now describes the hand well: 3-card heart support, extra values, length in both minors.

A double by the opener is a different matter, and we recommend that this should be treated as competitive. The bidding may begin:

South	West	North	East
1♡	1♠	2♡	No
No	2♠	No	No
Dbl			

There are two reasons for this apparent inconsistency. First, if a double is for penalties the trumps lie *under* declarer, clearly a less attractive situation. Secondly, 2NT is required as a natural bid. There is no reason why South should not be free to try 2NT with this hand:

♠AQ   ♡AQ752   ◇K32   ♣1094

A competitive double would be in order on this type of hand:

♠6   ♡KJ94   ◇AQ32   ♣A876

South did not want to advance further over 2♡, but he knows he can do better than defend 2♠. A competitive double should solve the problem: if North has 4-card heart support he will bid 3♡, and if not he can introduce a 4-card minor.

A rather different situation arises if responder did not have the option of making a penalty double on the previous round:

South	West	North	East
1♡	No	2♡	2♠
No	No	Dbl	

Again, a penalty double is unattractive with a weak hand sitting under the bidder. The best use for this type of double is to show a maximum raise with fair defensive values but not very good trumps, such as:

♠64   ♡A83   ◇K1084   ♣J1065

North is unwilling to sell out just yet, and a double is the best move. Here are three possible hands which South may hold:

(a)	♠Q85	(b)	♠75	(c)	♠AJ9
	♡KQJ62		♡KQ96		♡K764
	◇A72		◇AQ75		◇A73
	♣Q4		♣A32		♣K94

With hand (a) he pushes on to 3♡, which he should just make, and even if he is defeated it costs less than defending 2♠. With (b) he bids 3◇, which he makes comfortably, whereas 3♡ is considerably less secure. With (c), South will be happy to pass for penalties, and should set the contract at least one trick, probably two.

So far in this section we have been looking at hands on which the intervening side have not found a fit but have not actively disagreed. If they have bid two suits, other considerations arise:

South	West	North	East
1♡	1♠	2♡	3♣
Dbl			

This double is too valuable in its normal penalty sense to allocate it any conventional meaning. To bid as he has, East should have either a very good club suit, or a fair suit with spade support in reserve. South therefore should double with a hand which has good defence to clubs, is prepared to defend spades if partner holds them, and failing that can stand a retreat to 3♡. South may hold:

♠6 ♡AK753 ◇A842 ♣AJ9

If the double in the auction shown had come from North, after passes by South and West, the usual principle in such cases would apply: North is maximum for his first bid, has good defence to *spades* (the suit bid on his right), and invites South to pass for penalties if his hand is suitable. North could make this type of double with:

♠K107 ♡J84 ◇A9653 ♣86

The subject of doubling when only the opening side has found a fit is a tricky one, and the following summary may help to clarify the different situations.

When only one opponent has bid, a double by the player sitting over that opponent is a penalty suggestion which may be limited by the player's previous bidding. A double by the player sitting under the bidder is competitive, showing extra values, willingness to defend if partner holds the trumps, and at least one safe resting-place if not.

When both opponents have bid, a double by the player sitting over the bidder is for penalties, and may again be limited by earlier bidding. A double by the player sitting under the bidder shows strength in the *other* enemy suit, and is prepared to defend the bid suit if partner holds it.

(iii) The Defending Side Has Agreed a Suit

We call this type of competitive double the 'Snapdragon'. Look at South's dilemma in the following situation:

South	West	North	East
1◇	1♡	1♠	2♡
?			

South holds this everyday hand:

♠A4 ♡J103 ◇AKJ4 ♣QJ97

Any natural call contains a flaw: 3♣ suggests too much shape, 3♡ is far too pushing, 2NT might be ridiculous and 2♠ might work out well but might not. A pass would be virtually forcing, but would not offer North much assistance. The Snapdragon double is therefore used to convey the very precise message: 'I have values for another bid, but no natural call reflects my strength and distribution.' The bid implies tolerance for partner's suit, so North's decision on the next round should be a fairly easy one.

The following hand was a particularly happy example of the Snapdragon, from a large international pairs championship:

Dealer South, N-S Game

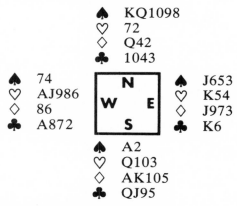

```
                    ♠  KQ1098
                    ♡  72
                    ◇  Q42
                    ♣  1043
  ♠  74                          ♠  J653
  ♡  AJ986      N                ♡  K54
  ◇  86       W   E              ◇  J973
  ♣  A872        S               ♣  K6
                    ♠  A2
                    ♡  Q103
                    ◇  AK105
                    ♣  QJ95
```

Generally the auction started like this:

South	West	North	East
1◇	1♡	1♠	2♡
2NT			

and whether North passed or raised to 3NT East-West were well content with this silly contract. Scores of −200 or −300 for North-South were almost universal, but there was one exception: on the second round one South produced the Snapdragon, and North rebid 2♠. Even though East-West found a club ruff, a score of +110 to North-South was worth a complete top.

The double can be used in exactly the same sense by the responding hand:

South	West	North	East
1◇	1♡	1♠	2♡
No	No	Dbl	

North may hold:

♠KJ63 ♡Q95 ◇86 ♣AJ32

What on earth is he to bid here without the double available? 2NT is suicidal with only Qxx in a bid and supported enemy suit; 3♣, a game-forcing reverse, is even worse; yet to pass when he knows his side holds more than half the high-card strength is unthinkable. The double copes with the hand perfectly, conveying the usual message: 'I don't want to give up yet, but I don't know where to go.' Here are some possible hands for South on the auction given:

(a) ♠Q82   (b) ♠Q5   (c) ♠7
    ♡64   ♡87   ♡J6
    ◇AQ53   ◇AK9754   ◇AQJ75
    ♣KQ76   ♣K65   ♣K9854

With hand (a) South gives delayed support to his partner's spades. North now bids 2NT, completing a very accurate description of his hand: about 11 points, something in hearts but not enough, only 4 spades. South bids 3♣, knowing the heart situation is too dangerous for no trumps, and North passes. On hand (b) South can only bid 3◇, and again North passes, reasonably certain of a 6-card suit opposite, since South has denied 3 spades, is unlikely to have more than 2 hearts on the bidding, and cannot bid clubs. On hand (c) South bids 3♣, and again North is happy to pass.

This particular type of double is normally played at the 2-level only: with no immediate fit and more than half the high cards, the opening side may well wish to take a penalty at the 3-level. But this is a matter of personal preference: if you find it easier on the memory to play all competitive doubles up to the 3-level you will not miss very much in the way of penalties, and it can be valuable to have the Snapdragon available on a hand such as:

♠Q7 ♡A4 ◇AK765 ♣KQ96

after the bidding has started with 1◇ from you, 1♡ on your left, 1♠ from partner and 3♡ on your right. Without the double available you would have to choose between gambling on 3NT and bidding 4♣, either of which might lead to a silly result.

(iv) Both Sides Have Agreed Suits

This is the time for the 'game-try double', one of the most valuable extensions of the competitive idea. The double is used where lack of bidding-space has robbed a player of the chance to make a traditional game try. This is the *locus classicus*:

South	West	North	East
1♠	2♡	2♠	3♡

Here 3♠ from South would be purely competitive, and a raise to 4♠ by North would be a 'double-cross'. Yet South may have a hand on which he is genuinely interested in game if his partner can co-operate, such as:

♠AQJ74 ♡J4 ◇AQ5 ♣A64

Without the 3♡ bid from East, this hand would merit a traditional trial bid of 3♣, but this has now been ruled out. A competitive 'game-try' double meets the case: the double by South in the auction given says, 'I should like to be in game if you are maximum for your original raise.'

This type of double may be converted into a penalty one if partner holds a suitable hand. If North in the situation described holds:

♠1043 ♡KQ10 ◇K3 ♣109874

he can see that 4♠ is a doubtful proposition, the heart values probably being wasted. Nevertheless, the defensive prospects are excellent: 3♡ should be defeated by at least two tricks and probably more.

Again, the double may be used in the same sense by the responder. In this sequence:

South	West	North	East
1♠	2♡	2♠	3♡
No	No	Dbl	

North has a maximum raise with only 3 trumps, and is prepared to compete once more. A hand on which he might double in this position is:

♠KJ4 ♡65 ◇A976 ♣J1032

and South with:

$$\spadesuit AQ965 \quad \heartsuit A72 \quad \diamondsuit K8 \quad \clubsuit Q54$$

would be justified in pushing on to game.

This concludes our examination of competitive doubles. You may feel that they depend too much on close partnership understanding. Perhaps – yet it is certainly true that the language of bidding is constantly becoming more sophisticated. It is by mastering an ever-increasing area of this language that a partnership will make itself very hard if not impossible to beat. Some of the doubling situations discussed in this chapter are very common indeed, and the natural penalty double simply does not occur in these positions. It is well worth discussing the most common cases with any fairly regular partner – the competitive double is becoming part of the everyday language of bidding, and by not using it a partnership puts itself at a disadvantage for no good reason.

9. The forcing pass

The forcing pass, if properly used, is one of the most valuable tools at your disposal in the competitive auction. But abuses are common, and can lead to ridiculous results. Who has not at least once in his career allowed opponents to play in an undoubled sacrifice because of a misunderstanding about a forcing pass?

A. AFTER LOW-LEVEL PENALTY DOUBLES

Generally, if you double the opponents in a low-level contract you are suggesting that you will not allow them to play the hand undoubled, meaning that you will either double their rescue or attempt to buy the contract for your side. An understanding of this kind is very helpful in cases where you are too strong to pass, yet your trump holding is not strong enough for a penalty double. You may suspect that your partner is waiting to double, but you cannot do it for him. What you need is to be able to pass, inviting him to double if he can, but with the proviso that if he cannot he will call something. Of course, sometimes your partner may decide to ignore the forcing pass because it appears too risky to re-enter the auction; so if your hand is exceptionally strong it may be better to make some normal forcing bid.

There are numerous situations in which the forcing pass can be applied. For example, as South you hold:

♠AQJ7 ♡AK754 ◇84 ♣A7

and the bidding has gone:

South	West	North	East
1♡	2♣	Dbl	2◇

(We are assuming that North has not had the benefit of reading our chapter on Sputnik, and that his double is the traditional penalty variety.) Here you clearly cannot double 2♢ yourself with nothing in trumps, but it would be a mistake to re-enter the fray now with a natural reverse of 2♠ – the hand may be a complete misfit, partner holding something like:

♠98   ♡6   ♢AJ953   ♣Q10842

This is the sort of deal where no one can make anything, and you want to defend. The slaughter in 2♢ doubled will be quite horrible, and it is essential to have the simple understanding that a pass from you now is forcing.

Again, still sitting South, you hold:

♠AK764   ♡Q7   ♢A8   ♣AQ53

and you double an opening 1NT on your right. West rescues to 2♢, which your partner doubles, and when this comes back to West he redoubles (obviously a cry for help). East obligingly removes to 2♡, and the ball is back with you. Many players would double on principle here, correctly reasoning that their side has most of the big guns and incorrectly assuming that this will guarantee an adequate penalty from 2♡. In practice you may find yourself defending against a useful 4-4 heart fit and taking a miserly 100 – indeed, it is not unknown for such contracts to succeed when the defence becomes over-confident! Far better to pass, saying to your partner, 'Despite my good hand I am not sure that defending 2♡ is our best bet – what do you think?' Partner will certainly double if he has any sort of useful holding in hearts, but if not he should find a bid, enabling you to find a safe game in spades or no trumps.

A final example of this type of forcing pass: again you are South and you hold:

♠AQ53   ♡64   ♢K4   ♣AJ753

Your partner opens 1♡, East doubles, and you redouble, thinking that there is something funny about this pack. West now runs to 2♣, of all things, and when this comes round to you, you double in unemotional tones. East disappointingly retreats to 2♢. Again, it would be a blunder to make a 'rhythm double' here – East may be conning you with some sort of diamond one-suiter, and even if he is not you cannot be sure of a large enough penalty to compensate you for the game which you can no doubt make. Leave it to partner; he should know what to do.

There is one case of this type where a pass should not be played as forcing. This is when an opponent makes a *jump* rescue from a doubled contract, as in this sequence:

South	West	North	East
1NT	Dbl	Rdbl	2♣
Dbl	3♡	No	No

South will not pass here unless his hand is exceptionally unsuitable; nevertheless it would be foolish to double (or bid) out of irritation at the unsatisfactory turn events have taken after such a promising start. It may be annoying to lose 140, but it would be a great deal more annoying to lose 300 or, worse still, 530. South must be free to pass if he can see no future in the hand.

B.   PASSES OF SACRIFICE BIDS

When the opponents are clearly sacrificing against your game or slam, your failure to double is obviously forcing on your partner. The purpose of this type of forcing pass is to suggest to your partner that it might be more profitable to advance further than to accept the penalty. Thus a pass of a game-level sacrifice suggests that your hand is unsuitable for defence and that you have the extra values to consider a 5-level contract. A pass of a 5-level sacrifice may be a slam invitation, in which case as well as the extra values you need a control in the opponents' suit, preferably a void.

For example, you are South and hold:

♠AQ65   ♡J7532   ◇K106   ♣7

The bidding goes:

South	West	North	East
	3♣	Dbl	No
4♣	No	4♠	5♣
?			

This is a typical case: partner's double was for take-out, and your hand has very good playing strength in a major-suit contract. However, North may have had to stretch to get into the bidding over the opening pre-empt, and you cannot be sure he can make eleven tricks. Pass, inviting him to choose between pressing on to 5♠ and taking a safe plus from 5♣ doubled.

Again as South your hand is:

♠7 ♡AKQ854 ◇643 ♣AKQ

and the bidding proceeds:

South	West	North	East
2♡	No	3♡	3♠
4♣	4♠	5◇	5♠
?			

Obviously you can take a fair-sized penalty out of 5♠, and you have no guarantee of making 6♡. However, a double would be quite wrong: East's 5♠ bid has given you a chance to show your spade control by passing, and you should do so. This may be all your partner is waiting to hear if he holds, say:

♠95 ♡J73 ◇AKQ9 ♣10864

If you doubled 5♠ he would have to stand it, knowing of two spade losers, but when you show the spade control he can take a much happier view of the slam prospects. (It may be noted that East's 5♠ bid is ill judged: without it, South has to make an immediate decision whether or not to go for slam, and is unable to consult his partner. It is rarely wise to make an advance sacrifice over a cue-bid in the suit immediately below trumps.)

A final spectacular example: as South you hold:

♠AQJ1064 ♡Q64 ◇AQ74 ♣—

and are excited to hear your partner open 1♡. Unfortunately, opponents are quick to get in on the act:

South	West	North	Est
		1♡	No
2♠	3♣	3♠	6♣
6♠	No	No	7♣
?			

What is East up to? Is he naively expecting his ♣A to stand up, or is he playing a more cunning game, holding ♡A or ♡K? An unthinking South might now make a unilateral decision to let himself be pushed into the grand slam, thinking that his club void is an unpleasant surprise in store for East-West. But this is a needless risk. You can simply pass, obviously guaranteeing that there is no immediate club loser, and leaving the final decision to partner.

It is worth noting in passing that you could have made things easier for your side by bidding 6♡ rather than 6♠ on the previous round. There are two reasons for this: first, it will make it easier for your partner to judge that what you want from him is good hearts, not a top diamond; perhaps more important, it may enable him to suggest 7♡ as an alternative contract – it is a possible explanation of East's activities that he is void in hearts and intends to make a punishing Lightner double of 7♠!

C.   OTHER FORCING PASSES

We have discussed above the two most common types of forcing pass, but there are several other situations in which a pass is either obviously forcing or best played as forcing. One has already been noted:

South	West	North	East
1♣	No	1♡	2◇
No			

It greatly facilitates bidding exchanges if South's pass is played as forcing in this type of sequence – the reasoning behind this has already been explained. The reader is also reminded of the pass by a player who could have made a Sputnik double, which is virtually though not completely forcing.

One very obvious type occurs when a player passes in a game-forcing situation. For instance, you hold:

♠AQ6 ♡KJ9 ◇A87 ♣AK63

You open 2NT, partner bids 3♣ (Baron), and next hand butts in with 3◇. We are confident that most of the players in an average field would now consider they had a choice between 3NT and Double . . . but both of these are quite wrong. You have nothing to say that you have not said already, so pass. You would double with a hand of this type:

♠AQ6 ♡K7 ◇A1085 ♣AKJ3

where your defence is even better than your opening bid suggests, while 3NT would be in order on:

♠AQ6 ♡KJ9 ◇AQ3 ♣AJ104

when you know you need not fear the diamonds. With the first hand given, you should reason that your opponent may even have saved you from disaster. Suppose that your partner holds:

♠KJ54 ♡Q762 ◇5 ♣J954

If you double, he will pass and you will hardly collect more than +300; if you bid 3NT he will pass and you will almost certainly be defeated. If you pass, he will know that 3NT is likely to be unsafe, and will find another bid, probably 4♣, taking you to a safe game in 5♣ or even in one of the majors.

Similarly, you hold at Game All:

♠AK75 ♡Q93 ◇AKQ8 ♣AQ

You open 2♣, partner replies the inevitable 2◇, and next hand surprisingly says 3♡. This hand was dealt in a multiple teams event, and the first round of bidding was the same at many tables. Those who doubled collected +800 or +500, depending on whether or not they prevented declarer making his ♣K. Those who bid 3NT scored +660, and those who bid 3♠ usually incurred a well merited minus score. A pass brought home the bacon: partner's hand was:

♠943 ♡– ◇J107643 ♣J982

with 6◇ unbeatable as the cards lay.

The message conveyed by the forcing pass is usually: 'I know you will be bidding again, and I have nothing definite I want to say at present.' In some circumstances, however, the pass can contain more accurate inferences. Our last example comes from a pairs tournament, and presents the unusual spectacle of the same player making two consecutive forcing passes.

Dealer South, E-W Game

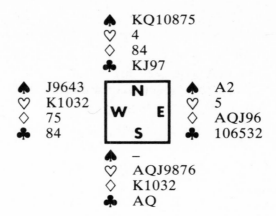

```
                    ♠ KQ10875
                    ♡ 4
                    ◇ 84
                    ♣ KJ97
   ♠ J9643          ┌─────────┐       ♠ A2
   ♡ K1032          │    N    │       ♡ 5
   ◇ 75             │ W     E │       ◇ AQJ96
   ♣ 84             │    S    │       ♣ 106532
                    └─────────┘
                    ♠ –
                    ♡ AQJ9876
                    ◇ K1032
                    ♣ AQ
```

Not surprisingly, this ferocious deal produced a wide variety of strange results. Of fourteen declarers, only one was successful – a North who was allowed to make 2♠ doubled. At one table the auction took this interesting course:

South	West	North	East
2♡(1)	No	2♠	Dbl(2)
No(3)	2NT(4)	Dbl(5)	3♣(6)
No(7)	No	Dbl	3◇(8)
Dbl	No	No	No

1) Normal Acol.
2) Better than 2NT – East has more defensive tricks than might be expected after such strong adverse bidding.
3) Forcing, of course, with a strong inference of bad spades (otherwise he would make his natural rebid) and very good hearts.
4) Possibly it was a pass in this position that allowed North to play 2♠ doubled.
5) Confirms that the hand is a misfit, and that a penalty will probably be the only way of making a plus score.
6) In case West has better clubs than diamonds. Redouble would certainly have been a better move.
7) Forcing again. South has now described his hand well: a pronounced 1-suiter in hearts, very bad spades, good defence

to diamonds but not to clubs. And he has still only made one bid!

8) Unwise, with the diamonds surely over him and the clubs under him . . . but it makes little difference now.

South did well in the defence, leading a trump, rising with ♣A at trick 2, and leading ♣Q to his partner's ♣K for a second trump lead. North-South eventually collected +800, even better than making 2♠ doubled.

10. Other competitive situations

In this chapter we shall try to 'pick up the pieces', examining those aids to competitive bidding which cannot be conveniently pigeon-holed in one of the preceding chapters. We shall begin with one of the most flexible and interesting – the cue-bid of the opponents' suit (or one of their suits) in competition.

Cue-Bids in Competition
In a previous chapter we looked at some of the conventional meanings that could be attached to an immediate cue-bid in opener's suit. We now have to consider what happens when the bid is made at a later stage of the auction. This is the simplest case:

South	West	North	East
1♣	1♡	2♡	

North here is simply saying that he wishes to be in game and has no other obvious bid. He is not promising a guard, half-guard or control of any kind in West's hearts; he is most likely to have either a hand suitable for 3NT but without good enough hearts, or massive support for clubs with a heart control and no good side suit. Any of the following hands would be suitable for the 2♡ bid:

(a) ♠KJ7   (b) ♠A6   (c) ♠K75
     ♡954   ♡A82   ♡K62
     ◇AQ6   ◇K94   ◇AQ103
     ♣K873   ♣AQ763   ♣J97

Hand (a) would present a real problem without the cue-bid – no raise in clubs describes the hand adequately, and one would have to resort to a bid in a 3-card suit, or a high-power Sputnik double if in use, either of which risks misinforming partner about the distribution. Hand (b) offers obvious prospects of a slam in clubs, and a double is the most helpful first move. Hand (c) could be handled by a Sputnik double, but if these are not being used a cue-bid will meet the case – a bid of 2◇, even if played as forcing, would sound too much like a 5-card suit, and a shy at no trumps now would obviously be premature.

The opener should rebid naturally over the cue-bid, but should give priority to bidding no trumps if he has the enemy suit well held, as this is doubtless what responder wishes to hear about.

An interesting question which rarely seems to be discussed in the text books is what the cue-bid should mean when used by a passed hand. We suggest the following scheme: if opener's suit is a major, the cue-bid shows a raise to at least 3 of the major, with a singleton in opponents' suit; if it was a minor, the cue-bid shows the values for 2NT without an adequate holding in opponents' suit. These otherwise idle bids thus become useful additions to the competitive armoury.

Moving one place round the table, we can identify two different situations in which fourth hand might cue-bid on the first round:

South	West	North	East
1♣	1♡	No/2♣	2♣/3♣

(We will ignore for the moment the case where North bids a third suit, giving East a choice of cue-bids.) In the two sequences shown, East's bid is the so-called 'Unassuming Cue-Bid', discussed fully in an earlier chapter. East needs to differentiate between this hand:

♠K72 ♡8432 ◇QJ75 ♣10

where he would like to bounce to 3♡ for pre-emptive effect, and this:

♠KQ8 ♡QJ87 ◇A943 ♣102

where he again wants to bid 3♥, but this time with hopes of game if partner has a sound overcall. The U.C.B. allows this distinction to be made: East bids 3♥ on the hand devoid of defensive tricks, and cue-bids the enemy suit on the constructive hand. Note that this arrangement in no way debars him from making a more traditional use of the cue-bid on the rare occasion when he has something like this:

♠A75 ♥K9863 ♦KQ104 ♣A

and has high hopes of at least a small slam – here he again bids opponents' clubs at the minimum level, but makes a further effort over partner's sign-off.

The opener too can make use of the cue-bid at his second turn:

♠KJ94 ♥– ♦AQ63 ♣KQJ108

After 1♣ from you, 1♥ on your left and two passes, 2♥ is a better effort than a re-opening double. This rather uncommon use should show specifically a strong 3-suited hand with a void in opponents' suit. If your partner has been shut out of the auction with, say:

♠Q53 ♥872 ♦K9854 ♣62

he will be able to revise drastically his original evaluation of these modest assets, and will know he can safely compete in diamonds to a high level.

If his partner has bid over the overcall, the opener's cue-bid has its normal meaning – forcing to game, and in the first instance looking for a guard in the enemy suit:

♠AQ6 ♥1053 ♦AJ9 ♣AKQ7

Having sensibly preferred to open 1♣ rather than a scratchy 2NT, you want to be in game when the bidding proceeds 1♥ on your left, 1♠ from partner, No Bid on your right. 2♥ will produce a descriptive rebid from your partner – if he has 5 spades you can put him in the spade game, if he has the hearts held no trumps should play well, and failing that you may find a good enough club fit to make 5♣. There is however a slight difference when then overcall comes on opener's right:

South	West	North	East
1♣	No	1♡	2◇
3◇			

If a pass by South in this position is played as forcing, as we suggested earlier, then that will be the most sensible action on:

♠AJ6 ♡K4 ◇753 ♣AKQ108

A forcing pass is superior to a cue-bid in several ways: it allows the bidding to die below the level of 3NT if responder is weak, and it gives him more space to describe his hand if he is unsuitable for no trumps. The cue-bid in this position can therefore be allocated its old-fashioned meaning of strong support for partner with a control in the enemy suit:

♠K65 ♡AJ97 ◇A ♣KQJ74

After the auction given, this hand is too strong for a raise to 4♡, and 3◇ followed by energetic heart support gives a clearer picture.

Once the bidding has gone beyond 3NT, the cue-bid reassumes its traditional role. If the cue-bidder's side has agreed a suit, he shows a control and slam interest. If not, the cue-bid may be ambiguous, as on this hand from rubber bridge. South held:

♠Q9753 ♡A6 ◇AQ10872 ♣—

and the bidding took an exciting route:

South	West	North	East
1◇	4♣	5♣	No

There are two possible explanations of North's 5♣ bid: either he has diamond support and a hand too strong to bid a direct 5◇, or he is looking at a massive major two-suiter. In either case, South's hand has become tremendous, and the problem is to find a bid that caters for both eventualities. The answer, as so often, is another cue-bid: 6♣. If North now bids 6◇, showing the hand with big diamond support, South can raise to 7◇; and if North shows the major two-suiter, presumably with 6♡, South can bid 7♠. North in fact bid 6♡, holding:

♠AKJ64 ♡KQJ97 ◇K ♣A4

and South's conversion to 7♠ was doubled by an irate East, who felt that no self-respecting pair could mention their trump suit for the first time at the level of seven!

One conventional use of the cue-bid which seems to cause a great deal of confusion is the so-called 'directional asking bid', whereby a bid of the enemy suit below the level of 3NT asks partner to bid no trumps with *half* a guard in the enemy suit. This arrangement is liable to lead to an elegant 3NT with Jx facing Qx in the key suit, and is not recommended as a general treatment. Even if the joint guard is secure, you have told your opponents that you can only stop the suit once, and they will know whether to lead it or look elsewhere. However, there are instances in which the cue-bid may be properly used for this exact purpose by inference:

South	West	North	East
1◇	1♡	2♣	No
2◇	No	2♡	No
3♣	No	3♡	

North's 2♡ is a normal cue-bid, and South's preference to 3♣ denies an adequate guard in hearts. The 3♡ bid is clearly saying that a half-guard will do – North may hold:

♠A7 ♡J63 ◇K54 ♣AQJ87

When there is no space available for this type of second cue-bid, the same result may be achieved by different means:

South	West	North	East
1◇	2♣	3♣	No
3◇	No	3♡	

North is rather unlikely to hold a heart suit on this bidding, and a more probable explanation of his tactics is that he is still probing for 3NT. Certainly South should take this opportunity to bid 3NT with a half-guard in clubs.

A 'raise' of the cue-bid has a similar but subtly different meaning:

South	West	North	East
1◇	1♠	2♣	No
2♠	No	3♠	

In expert circles, the generally agreed meaning of North's 3♠ bid is, 'I do have something in spades, but not enough to bid no trumps myself; if you have a bolster in the suit, no trumps may be better played from your side.' He may hold:

♠A6　♡Q94　◇J75　♣AQ1032

when it is important for South to be declarer at no trumps if he holds something in spades such as Qxx.

A different approach occurs when opponents have bid two suits, so that a choice of cue-bids is available:

South	West	North	East
1◇	1♠	2♣	2♡
2♠/3♡			

The accepted rule here is that South is *promising* a guard in the suit he bids, not asking for one. Similarly:

South	West	North	East
1◇	No	1♠	Dbl
2♡			

East has in effect bid hearts, so South is unlikely to be suggesting that suit as a possible resting place. More likely, he has some such holding as:

♠Q7　♡AQ9　◇AKJ86　♣1043

and is showing his strong heart holding in the hope that North guards the clubs (the other suit implied by East's double) and can bid no trumps. It is hard to see what other bid South could make here if 2♡ is not available in this sense.

Occasionally, you may wish to try to play in a suit bid by opponents. Obviously this is not a common state of affairs, but that is no reason to ignore it. One familiar case arises when partner has bid no trumps over an enemy suit bid: now a bid of that suit by either partner is a suggestion that it may be a playable trump suit:

South	West	North	East
1♣	1♠	1NT	No
2♠			

When North has described his hand so accurately, 2♠ is not needed as a general-purpose force, and South should feel free to bid 2♠ on:

♠Q8653 ♡A10 ◇7 ♣AK975

It is not after all unknown for spade overcalls to be psychic.

Other cases (involving natural systems) are largely matters of common sense:

South	West	North	East
1♣	No	1♠	No
2♣	No	No	2♠

East has a spade suit – what else could he possibly be trying to say?

We should mention in this context the special problem that arises when your opponents are playing a 'canapé' system, such as Roman Club or Blue Club. In these systems the first suit bid is not necessarily the longest held, and in Roman Club it may even be a 3-card suit. We therefore recommend that against the Roman Club only, you should play immediate cue-bids of major suits as natural:

South	West	North	East
1♠	2♠		

South could well have only 3 spades, and if you do not play the direct cue-bid as natural you will find some hands impossible to bid.

With Blue Club, the opening bid is almost always at least a 4-card suit, but it is wise to retain an open mind about the possibility of playing in that suit. In the following auction, North-South are playing Blue Club:

South	West	North	East
1♠	No	1NT	No
2◇	Dbl		

West's second round double is for take-out, and should be prepared for his partner to bid spades.

We may summarize the various uses of the cue-bid in competition as follows:

(i) If the bidding can still stop in 3NT, and no suit has been agreed, the first cue-bid is a general-purpose force, and should initially be taken as asking for a guard in the enemy suit.

(ii) A raise of the type of cue-bid described in (i) asks for help in the suit, and suggests that partner should be declarer in no trumps.

(iii) Otherwise a second cue-bid below 3NT is a 'directional asking bid', looking for a half-guard in the suit.

(iv) If a major suit has been agreed by the cue-bidding side, the cue-bid may be an orthodox slam try in the suit, showing a control in the enemy suit, or may be a suggestion that no trumps would be better.

(v) If opponents have bid two suits, a cue-bid of either promises a guard in that suit, and asks by inference for a guard in the other.

(vi) Beyond the level of 3NT, a cue-bid is always a slam try.

B.   DEFENDING AGAINST ARTIFICIAL BIDS

There are some commonly used artificial bids which may cause problems to opponents who have not developed a clear partnership understanding about how to deal with them. In this section we shall consider some of the most frequently encountered problems of this kind. For instance:

South	West	North	East
1NT	No	2♣	Dbl

North's 2♣ is Stayman – an everyday situation. But are you sure, sitting West, that you know what your partner's double means? Has he got a strong club suit which he would like you to lead against an eventual no-trump contract, or is he simply saying that he has a good hand and would have doubled 1NT? Either method is playable, but it is prudent to agree on one or the other. The obvious advantage of reserving the double to show the strong hand is that you will not be shut out of the auction; but on grounds of frequency it may be better to play the double as lead-directing. Normally the strong hand will get a chance to bid on the second round, for example if the opener rebids in a major suit and the responder passes. And doubling on a strong hand can backfire nastily, as on this hand from the Hubert Phillips Bowl:

Dealer North, E-W Game

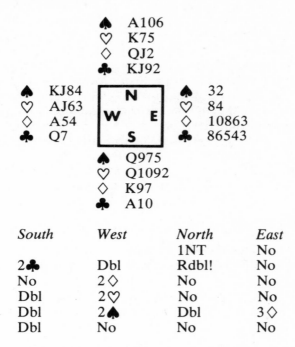

South	West	North	East
		1NT	No
2♣	Dbl	Rdbl!	No
No	2◇	No	No
Dbl	2♡	No	No
Dbl	2♠	Dbl	3◇
Dbl	No	No	No

North and South both showed good judgement in this auction, North in redoubling 2♣ to suggest that it might be a playable contract, and South in passing the redouble (no defence beats 2♣). East might have saved his side a few hundred by bidding 2◇ over the redouble: he was correct in pointing out that 2◇ doubled is more expensive than 2♣ redoubled . . . but he could hardly expect his partner to know that! North-South were not extended in taking a 1400 penalty after a trump lead, and the match was virtually over. It is fair to say that this hand is not so much an argument against doubling on strong hands as a reminder that strong hands should *be* strong: a scattered 15-count is not a sound double of a weak 1NT.

Many tournament partnerships nowadays play transfer

responses to a 1NT opening, and there is a standard defence to these which should be in your repertoire. After this bidding:

South	West	North	East
1NT	No	2♦	

where 2♦ is announced as a transfer to hearts, East should double to show diamonds and bid 2♥ – the real enemy suit – for take-out.

The Unusual No Trump is another weapon that can be turned against its user with a properly organized defence. After, let us say, a 1♥ opening from partner and a 2NT overcall on your right, showing the minors, the recommended method is: double to show interest in defending a minor-suit contract; bid 3♣ with 3-card support for partner's hearts and 4 spades; bid 3♦ with 3-card heart support and 5 spades.

When a 1NT opening is followed by artificial intervention, such as an Aspro 2♣, the bidding becomes fraught with interesting traps for both sides. The following methods work well in practice. The responder to 1NT should double if he has good defence to the suit the overcaller has shown *and* adequate defence to the suit actually bid. After partner's 1NT has been overcalled with an Aspro 2♣ (promising hearts), double with:

♠K75 ♥AJ62 ♦Q98 ♣J76

but not with:

♠KJ76 ♥AJ852 ♦Q94 ♣2

where you may catch a nasty cold defending 2♣ doubled. The best action on such hands is to pass, and the 1NT opener should generally re-open if the artificial bid is passed round to him.

A bid of the suit opponents have shown is forcing to game: opener should repeat no trumps with a guard in the enemy suit, or bid the other major if he has 4 of it, failing that bid a minor suit. If the overcall has promised two suits you can follow normal principles by bidding the one in which you have a guard:

♠KQ7 ♥J9 ♦K652 ♣A1076

After 1NT from your partner and 2♣ on your right, bid 2♥ if the overcall was Aspro, but 2♠ if it was any version that purports to show *both* majors.

As for the partner of the conventional overcaller, he should bid naturally. The only special understanding worth adopting here is that if the overcall is doubled, a pass should show willingness to play there if partner happens to hold the suit he has bid, while a redouble suggests that you are happy with the contract even if partner holds two other suits. Thus after 1NT on your left, 2♣ (Aspro) from partner, Double on your right, it is best to pass with:

♠K953 ♡J7 ♢A982 ♣Q64

but redouble with:

♠75 ♡A2 ♢K965 ♣QJ1083

Over any 2-level intervention after 1NT, we recommend that a raise to 2NT be played as purely competitive: opener should not bid game, though he may remove to a 5-card suit (presumably a minor) if that looks more satisfactory. Responder should have some help in the enemy suit, of course, even if as little as 10xx or a doubleton honour.

One of the authors has evolved a scheme of transfers for dealing with a 2♠ overcall after 1NT, the bid that normally causes most difficulty at the table. It works like this:

South	West	North	East
1NT	2♠	?	

2NT from North is competitive as usual. 3♣ is a transfer to 3♢, over which North may pass (with a long diamond suit), bid 3♡ with 4 of them, bid 3♠ to show at least 4-4 in the minors, or continue to 3NT with game values and a good diamond suit but no spade guard.

3♢ shows a heart suit, and if opener has nothing further to say he simply bids 3♡ and awaits developments. If he still likes the look of 3NT, he bids 3♠ with half a guard in spades and 3NT with a full guard; if he is happy with hearts he can raise to game, or cue-bid a minor-suit ace if his hand is particularly suitable. This arrangement allows responder to bid 3♡ himself over the intervention if he simply wishes to compete – this should always be passed. Finally, North can bid 3♠ to show a good club suit but no spade guard.

C.   ESCAPING FROM 1NT DOUBLED

Particularly at pairs, it is rarely a good idea to play in 1NT doubled. If you are going to make it, you may as well redouble; if not, it will probably be no more expensive, and will often be cheaper, to run to a suit – a 4-3 or better fit must exist somewhere. Following this reasoning, some tournament players now use a compulsory redouble of 1NT when a double on the opener's left is passed back to him. Several different methods of wriggling are in use, but the following works as well as any and has the virtue of simplicity. When 1NT is doubled, the opener's partner if weak should take the following action:

(i)   With a 5-card or longer suit, he bids it at once, and opener must pass.

(ii)   With 4 clubs and another 4-card suit, he redoubles. Opener must bid 2♣ unless he has only 2 of them (or 3 in a 4-3-3-3 shape) in which case he bids 2♢ and responder either passes or bids his major.

(iii)   With two 4-card suits other than clubs, responder passes and opener must redouble, over which responder bids his lower-ranking suit. If this bid is 2♡, opener picks a major; if 2♢, opener bids 2♡ with a doubleton diamond or 4-4 in the majors, otherwises passes.

(iv)   With any 4-3-3-3, he passes, and bids 2♣ over the redouble.

If responder is strong, of course, he passes, and leaves in the redouble. This escape mechanism is admittedly a little risky at teams or rubber bridge, but can produce excellent results at pairs, especially against weak opposition, who may find it difficult to untangle the subsequent bidding, and decide to go for a contract themselves instead of doubling you.

11. Defence to pre-empts

In this chapter we shall be studying the best methods of counter-ing the considerable difficulties caused by high-level opening bids – that is, all bids from 2♣ upwards which carry no sugges-tion of strength.

A. THE WEAK THREE

We start with the most common form of pre-emption, the weak opening of 3 of a suit, normally played as showing a good 7-card suit with nothing outside. It cannot be denied that such bids frequently achieve their object of making it impossible for opponents to find their best fit in time. Numerous conventional defences have been devised, but none is anywhere near perfect. To begin with, we shall assume that you are going to play a double as for take-out: this is far from being the most popular method in British bridge, but it gives us a simple and convenient place from which to start. In fact the penalty double of a weak three is not very valuable: it is rare for an opponent to have the type of hand on which he can at once say with confidence, 'I think our best bet is to defend this.'

How strong, then, and of what type should your hand be to intervene after a weak three? It is impossible to give a general answer to this question, as there are a number of factors that must be taken into consideration.

The basic requirement is that you should have at least moder-ate support for all the unbid suits. As in other take-out double situations, 3 cards to an honour may be considered adequate, and you should place greater emphasis on the unbid majors than on the minors.

The strength required depends on the level at which you may be forcing partner to bid, on the vulnerability, and on your position at the table. For instance, a take-out double of an opening 3♣ when you are second to speak (that is, your partner has not yet passed) requires little more than normal opening values. But if the opening was in a major suit, so that you have to be prepared for a response at the 4-level, you will need an extra trick. If you are vulnerable, safety decrees that you should have a little extra strength, or at least *good* support for all the unbid suits. Again, if your partner has already passed there is more to be lost than gained by borderline doubles of enemy pre-empts, so once more extra values are required.

Consider the following example hands:

(a)	♠KJ105	(b)	♠94	(c)	♠K1073
	♡AJ3		♡Q73		♡K4
	◇A10742		◇AKQ7		◇AQ63
	♣7		♣KQJ3		♣KJ4

Holding hand (a), you hear a 3♣ opening on your right, and you are not vulnerable. You have little more than a minimum opening bid, but otherwise everything is in your favour, and you should certainly double. With hand (b), you face a very different situation: you are vulnerable, your partner has passed, and the opening bid on your right is 3♠. You have a very much stronger hand than (a), but even so you should pass. Your support for the unbid major is tenuous, and silence here must be the lesser risk. Of course, you may miss a game by passing; but you are too likely to incur a four-figure penalty by bidding.

On hand (c), you are again vulnerable, and again partner has passed, the opening bid this time being 3♡. This is a borderline hand, despite the good spade support. If your left-hand opponent has also passed, you are worth a double; if not, it is just a little too dangerous, and you should pass.

The rules governing the strength required to intervene are flexible, and you must rely largely on your judgement, taking into consideration the state of the rubber (or match), the calibre of the opposition and your partner's skill in card-play. It should also be noted that we have so far been discussing only the question of intervention 'under the gun' – that is, when the pre-empt has been bid on your right. In the remote or protective position, intervention can be a good deal more flimsy. With this hand:

♠AJ97 ♡KJ532 ◇Q72 ♣8

it would be overbold to double an opening 3♣ on your right; but if the bid is opened on your left and passed back to you, you would earn censure if you kept your peace. Most of the time you should be prepared to sniff things out at the table, sensing danger on some hands, a green light on others. Above all, you must accept that you will be talked out of something by a pre-empt from time to time. On the other hand, if it is your proud boast that you have never conceded an 800 penalty in contesting against a 3-bid, the probability is that you are being too timid.

If the double is used as for take-out, all other bids may be used in their natural sense. To overcall in a suit at the minimum level shows a fair hand with a good suit, the strength being controlled by the old 'rule of 500'. This is a dictum dating from the days of Culbertson, stating that you should not risk losing more than 500 points by any action you may take. Thus if vulnerable you should be within two tricks of your bid; if not vulnerable, within three tricks. An overcall of 3NT is natural, possibly showing a balanced rock-crusher, but more often a hand with a running minor suit and a bit of hope. Cue-bidding the enemy suit will take the bidding to the sky-level very rapidly, and you should only resort to it on a two-suited hand of immense playing strength. Below are three examples of hands which would not be suitable for a take-out double after an opposing opening of 3♡ on your right:

(a) ♠KQ9632 (b) ♠J   (c) ♠AKJ1073
     ♡A6   ♡K104   ♡5
     ◇KQ62   ◇AKQ963   ◇AKQ84
     ♣7   ♣AQ5   ♣A

With hand (a) you call 3♠ at any vulnerability – provided partner has one or two trumps for you, you can hardly lose more than 500. Hand (b) justifies a 3NT overcall . . . yes, you may miss a slam in a minor suit, but you should be content to bid what you can reasonably expect to make. Hand (c) is the rare monster that justifies a cue-bid of the pre-empter's suit.

If the pre-emptive opening is in a minor suit, special problems arise. Paradoxically, this lower-level pre-empt is more difficult to handle, which is why good players tend to be much less disciplined with their 3-bids when the long suit is a minor. The position can be summed up like this: if you have a strong, fairly balanced hand and the player on your right opens 3♡, intervention by you will probably lead either to 3NT or to 4♠, and partner should be able to help you decide which; but if the opening is 3♢, game in *either* major is still a possibility. Holding:

$$♠K1032 \qquad ♡76 \qquad ♢AKJ9 \qquad ♣A53$$

you would certainly intervene with a double of 3♡ . . . but a 3♣ opening is much more of a problem. If you double, partner is almost sure to bid 3♡, and whatever you do now may lead to an idiotic result. A take-out double of a minor-suit pre-empt should be prepared for either major, or be sufficiently strong to make a further bid next round.

The responder to the double often has to say his piece at the 4-level, and there cannot therefore be very much precision in his reply. Simply consider the type of hand your partner is likely to hold, and try to select a sensible contract. You may bid a suit at the minimum level with up to two tricks in your hand. With a fair 5-card suit and two tricks or more you can bid game, especially in a major, even if this means jumping the bidding. To bid 3NT you need, obviously, a secure guard in the enemy suit, as well as a few fillers outside.

A penalty pass of the take-out double does not require the very strong trump holding needed for such action at the 1-level. With a fair defensive hand which includes a trump trick but no reasonable suit you should usually pass, because, even with 26 or more points between you, it is easy to miss your best fit when your investigations have to start at such a high level.

A cue-bid of the enemy suit can be a useful move on a good hand which cannot choose a suit, though only when there is room to do so below the game level. In general it is a mistake to worry too much about missing slams after a pre-emptive bid: if there is a clear road ahead by which you can unambiguously display your extra values, well and good; but if investigation means an adventure at the 5-level on a borderline hand, then let the slam go a-begging.

A few example hands will clarify the options open to the responder to a take-out double of an opening three-bid. On the first three, your partner has doubled an opening 3♠ on your left:

	(a)	(b)	(c)
♠	76	76	7
♡	Q853	AQ853	Q8
◇	Q85	Q85	Q8532
♣	8532	852	KJ852

Both (a) and (b) offer no sensible alternative to a bid of 4♡, the main difference being that with (b) you expect to make it. With hand (c) the best bid if 4NT, showing the minor-suit values – some would choose 4♠, but now a response of 5♡ leaves you no-where to go. If partner takes your 4NT as Blackwood, shoot him.

On the next three hands the situation is the same except that the opening bid was 3♡:

	(a)	(b)	(c)
♠	K4	QJ754	A87
♡	A72	A7	QJ5
◇	K8643	864	9864
♣	753	753	753

Hand (a) is suitable for a response of 3NT: the unsupported ace may seem a shaky protection against a 7-card suit, but you can hold it up long enough to exhaust your right-hand opponent of hearts, and the pre-empter is unlikely to have anything else to regain the lead. On hand (b) you have an obvious jump to 4♠. Hand (c) is typical of the sort of hand that should pass the double for penalties: you have two defensive tricks and no guarantee of making anything your way.

Alternative Defences

We have examined the take-out double as a defence to three-bids, and established the type of hand that should compete and the options open to responder. Now we can look at some of the alternative defences popular in Britain. These all have the obvious (if sometimes overstated) advantage that a double can be used in a natural sense, for penalties; against that one has as usual to weigh the loss of the bid being used as conventional.

3NT for take-out is perhaps the most popular method among rank-and-file players, and is not quite as bad as its detractors make out. But it has the disadvantage of taking the bidding to the 4-level, and is particularly space-consuming after a minor-suit pre-empt. It also makes it difficult for its users to alight in 3NT when that happens to be the right contract, as is quite frequently the case. True, fourth hand may convert a penalty double to 3NT, but there is often some doubt in this position as to who, if anyone, holds the enemy suit. (It is of course most unwise to allow the partner of the 3NT bidder to pass the bid, as the reluctant declarer is likely to have a completely unsuitable hand.)

Lower Minor is a more practical defence, in that the bids used as take-out requests (3 ◇ over 3 ♣, 4 ♣ over everything else) are not much missed in their natural sense. Once again, though, the 4 ♣ bid takes the auction rather high, and leaves responder no space to say whether his hand is good or bad.

Fishbein (sometimes misnamed 'Herbert') is the most economical defence in terms of bidding-space, other than the take-out double. The idea here is that the next suit up is always the take-out request (4 ♣ over 3 ♠). However, the loss of a natural 3 ♡ over 3 ◇ or 3 ♠ over 3 ♡ is not to be lightly borne: it is infuriating to hold:

♠7   ♡AKJ965   ◇K43   ♣652

and to hear a 3 ◇ opening on your right, so that you cannot make your natural 3 ♡ bid for fear that partner will bid large numbers of spades. This defence cannot really be regarded as very sound.

Film is a thoughtful attempt to improve Fishbein by combining it with Lower Minor (hence the name). Fishbein is used normally, except that the 3 ♡ and 3 ♠ take-outs guarantee at least 4 cards in the suit bid; lacking this requirement, the take-out request over 3 ◇ or 3 ♡ is always 4 ♣.

Reese is the defence sometimes known as x-3-x, consistently advocated by Terence Reese in his books on bidding theory. By this method, 3NT is for take-out if the hand on your right opens with 3 of a major, but in all other situations a double is for take-out. A modification known as x-4-x uses 4♣ as the take-out request immediately over 3 of a major, so that 3NT is always available as a natural bid. Both these methods are clearly better than the simpler ones, though it must be said that minor pre-empts are often weaker than major-suit ones, so that the loss of the penalty double can result in missing the occasional big killing.

D-x-C-x is identical to x-4-x except that the take-out request after a 3♣ opening on your right is 3♢ instead of a double. This is perhaps the most efficient – or least inefficient – of the standard defences, as it retains all the useful natural bids except the penalty double of 3♢, and is also economical of space.

Optional Double is a favourite death-trap. Most players who announce this defence mean in effect that they reserve the right to double with trumps or without trumps, and partner is expected to guess which. The optional double is correctly used as a part of D-x-C-x and the similar defences, sitting *under* the pre-emptive bidder – now a double shows a strong balanced hand with defensive tricks, and partner is expected to pass with a trick or two in trumps. But this type of double should not be used when the pre-empt is on your right, as if partner does have trumps they will now be badly placed.

In summary, we feel it is safe to say that the optional double is the best defence for the player sitting under the pre-emptive opener. Whatever defence you are using in the immediate position, it is useful to be able to pass when you hold good trumps and nothing else, knowing that if partner has the defensive values to beat the contract he will re-open with a double. A problem does arise however when in the optional double position you hold a good 3-suited hand with a void in opener's suit, such as:

♠– ♡AK64 ♢QJ872 ♣AQ95

Now when 3♠ on your left is followed by two passes, a double may work out badly if partner holds:

♠K105 ♡J832 ♢K96 ♣K43

and quite reasonably passes for penalties. You are unlikely to defeat 3♠ doubled by more than one trick, and it may easily be makable, while 4♡ your way is unlikely to be defeated. It is well worth considering the advantages of playing Lower Minor as a distributional take-out request in this position.

In the immediate position it is not so easy to be dogmatic. Over 3♣, 3♢ seems the best take-out bid, allowing plenty of room for responder to describe his hand but retaining the option of the penalty double. Over 3♢, the choice seems to lie between a take-out double and the Film idea, or perhaps a variation of Film whereby 3♡ and 3♠ are *both* for take-out, showing 4 cards in the suit bid, while 4♣ is available for hands with both majors which are unsuitable for no-trump play even if partner holds the diamonds. Over 3♡ or 3♠, 4♣ for take-out appears the most practical solution. The only certainty is that, whichever defence you play, you will sometimes wish you had settled on something else. . . .

B.   THE WEAK TWO

The use of the Weak Two opening is increasing in popularity: it is standard in several of the One Club systems, and has also been grafted on to Acol by many tournament players who use the form of that system known as 'Benjaminized'. It is a half-pre-emptive, half-constructive opening, which shows a fair 6-card suit and a point-count inadequate for an opening one-bid. Under English Bridge Union rules, the Weak Two must have a range of no more than 5 points: thus some pairs play 6-10, some 7-11, some vary it according to vulnerability. The bid is useful if restricted to the type of hand for which it was designed; holding, say:

♠KJ10864   ♡72   ♢A43   ♣98

you feel it would be timid to say nothing, but it is dangerous to devalue the opening one-bid too far, and an opening 3♠ involves obvious risks.

As with opening three-bids, it is sensible to use a double of a weak two in the protective position as 'optional', showing a fairly strong balanced hand with only a moderate trump holding. Whatever your favoured defence, it is useful to have another bid available in the protective position for hands on which you would not welcome a penalty pass of the double, and for this purpose we recommend the Hackett convention, whereby 3♣ is a moderate take-out bid and 3◇ a strong one. The most popular defences when sitting immediately over the Weak Two bidder are the take-out double and the 3♣-3◇ arrangement mentioned above.

(a) ♠KQ72	(b) ♠KQ72	(c) ♠KQ72
♡–	♡106	♡A
◇AJ953	◇AJ95	◇AKJ95
♣Q762	♣KQ7	♣KQ7

After an opening 2♡ on your left is passed round to you, hand (a) is one where you feel some action is justified but a protective double would be too dangerous: it is highly likely that partner has some trumps, and if he passes for penalties the result could be embarrassing. A take-out of 3♣ should lead to a playable contract. With hand (b) a double is clearly superior, and a penalty pass will not cause you any pain. Hand (c) is far too good to want to defend 2♡ doubled, and here a strong take-out of 3◇ is in order.

If you were sitting immediately over the opener, your action would depend on the defence being used: playing double for take-out, you would probably double on all three; otherwise you would bid 3♣ on (a) and (b) and 3◇ on (c).

Except against very irresponsible opponents, we consider that it does not pay to use the double for penalties, and we shall therefore proceed on the assumption that in the immediate position you will play a double as for take-out. The type of hand required is similar to that for a one-level double, except that for safety reasons you need 2-3 points more as a minimum, as you will normally be committing your side to the 3-level. As with opening three-bids, there are situations where it is safe to compete even on moderate hands without too much risk of punishment. If the opening two-bid was made third in hand it is unlikely that opponents will be able to do you too much harm, as your side is almost certain to have at least half the points. Similarly in other positions you should be more prepared to risk intervention if your partner has not passed than if he were the dealer.

Responding to this type of double is similar to responding to a normal take-out double at the 1-level, except that (as with 3-bids) you may more readily pass on a moderate trump holding: as little as QJ9x will do if the rest of your hand looks good for defence. Jump responses, either in a suit or in no trumps, carry the same meaning as at the lower level – a fair suit and about one and a half tricks in the one case, 10-11 points with a guard in opponents' suit in the other. On game-going hands the answer is very often a cue-bid of opponents' suit, promising nothing in particular and asking the doubler to make a descriptive rebid.

C.   OTHER PRE-EMPTIVE BIDS

(i) 2♣ Natural
Most 1♣ systems include a 2♣ opening bid on a limited hand with a long club suit, a bid which is sometimes pre-emptive in effect if not in intention. The best defence to this is simple: double for take-out, other bids natural. The player sitting under the 2♣ bidder should always be prepared to have his double passed for penalties – with a hand unsuitable for this, 3♣ is available. It is worth noting that many one-clubbers are rather vague about coping with intervention over this opening, so that it can pay to take greater risks than usual.

(ii) Precision 2◇
An awkward bid to combat is the old-style Precision 2◇ opening on a three-suited hand with short diamonds. The best tactic is to use a double to show a diamond suit; hands with good defence to two or three suits should pass and await developments. To make a natural suit overcall is obviously very dangerous, and the best use for the immediate overcall is to show a two-suited hand, with the suit bid plus diamonds. In the unlikely event that 2◇ is passed round to fourth hand, he should of course protect on practically any thirteen cards.

(iii) Multicoloured 2◇
This opening is currently enjoying a considerable vogue, due almost entirely to the difficulty of defending against it. Make no mistake – it is essential to have an adequate defence prepared. Even if only one pair in your area uses the convention, you will

have trouble against them unless you are quite sure what you are doing.

Several versions of the 'Multi' exist. Normally, however, a 2♢ opening shows either a Weak Two in an unspecified major, or some kind of strong hand – exactly what kind need not concern us, as if you intervene over the strong version you will almost certainly regret it. The responder to the opening usually bids 2♡, but with considerably better hearts than spades may bid 2♠. 2NT is a strong inquiry. Higher responses are not much used, one of the disadvantages being that responder is reluctant to pre-empt in case his partner is strong.

In planning a defence, then, we must consider three main possibilities: (a), action when 2♢ is opened on your right; (b), action when 2♢ is bid on your left and 2♡ on your right; and (c), action when the bid on your right is 2♠.

When 2♢ is opened on your right, it does not pay to make natural one-suited overcalls in the majors, because of the risk that your suit may be opener's as well. We therefore recommend that in this position 2♡ and 2♠ be played as mainly for take-out, with at least 4 cards in the suit bid and not more than a doubleton in the other major. With preparation for both majors (4-3 or better) you can double, which will sometimes result in taking a penalty – partner will know what to do. 2NT in this position is a natural bid on a strong balanced hand (15-18) with no particular reference to guards in the majors. Other bids are natural.

After the bidding in front of you has proceeded 2♢-No-2♡, you still know little about your opponents' hands. Holding the hearts, you should pass: if 2♡ goes round to your partner he should usually protect with a double, or if opener converts to 2♠ you can double when this comes back to you. An immediate double of the 2♡ response shows spades and should be prepared for a penalty pass – with a more distributional hand, of course, you can bid 2♠ yourself.

After 2♢-No-2♠, you now know that your right-hand opponent has a distinct preference for hearts over spades. In this position, a double from you shows hearts, and should again be prepared for a penalty pass. With spades, you wait – it is now likely that this suit is opener's long one. If opener really has hearts, you can show your spades by doubling on the next round.

To summarize the action you should take when 2 ◇ is opened on your left: pass when you hold the suit bid on your right, double with the other major.

The methods outlined above should handle the problem of the Multi effectively enough. It will score its occasional successes, but most of the outright disasters suffered against it at present are the result of inadequate preparation.

(iv) Pre-Emptive 2NT

One is unlikely to wish to argue with a natural 2NT, but some tournament pairs now use this opening to show a pre-emptive three-bid in an unspecified minor (this fits in with those systems in which 3♣ and 3 ◇ are strong openings). The defence to this is clear cut: double with good defensive values and no particular enthusiasm for the majors; bid 3♣ with a hand suitable for take-out containing 4 or more hearts; and 3 ◇ with a similar hand, 4 or more spades and fewer than 4 hearts (this reflects a common trend in expert bidding of using clubs as a cipher for hearts, diamonds for spades – the South African Texas openings are a case in point). After 2NT on your left, 3♣ on your right, double with good defence to diamonds, and bid 3 ◇ for take-out. If the bid on your right is 3 ◇, suggesting bad diamonds and better clubs, double for take-out.

(v) 3♣ Natural

A few systems, most importantly Blue Club, use 3♣ as a fairly strong opening bid, showing about 7 playing tricks and a very good club suit. A double of this should be strictly for take-out in any position, as a worth-while penalty is very unlikely.

(vi) Gambling 3NT

In the modern game, a 3NT opening normally shows a solid minor suit with not more than a queen outside. A double of this opening is for penalties, and should be based either on a solid suit of one's own, or on the knowledge that opener's minor suit will not run. With a hand such as this:

♠AQ654 ♡KQ108 ◇6 ♣AK6

it is a waste of time to double – the opener's partner will know whether 3NT can be made or not, so you can hardly gain by the bid. The best action on such hands is to bid 4 of a minor for take-out – 4♣ stressing hearts and 4♦ stressing spades. After 3NT on your left and the standard rescue of 4♣ on your right, the best tactic is to double with a strong all-round hand that is prepared to defend 4 of either minor, and bid 4♦ with a big distributional hand which wishes to be in game.

(vii) High-Level Pre-Empts

When the opponents open the bidding at the 4- or 5-level, there can naturally be little precision in constructive bidding. However, we must establish some principles relating to the meaning of doubles and take-out bids in the various positions. The double of an opening 4♣ or 4♦ should be construed as being primarily for take-out, but responder will only remove it if he has a reasonable suit of his own. It is necessary to abandon any idea of playing in delicate 4-4 fits on these occasions unless you are prepared to risk landing in some ludicrous contracts from time to time.

If, as is common in tournament play, the 4♣ and 4♦ openings are ciphers for the majors (South African Texas), the double should show a strong hand primarily interested in penalties but with at least 3 cards in the 'unbid' major.

Similarly, to double an opening bid of 4♡ you need a strong hand with at least tolerance for spades – three cards headed by a top honour would be about the minimum unless the hand was exceptionally powerful. Over 4♠, a double is best played as purely for penalties, as you can call 4NT without loss of bidding space if you want partner to choose a suit. However, 4NT should only be bid with impeccable distribution and considerable power, as you are surrendering the option of taking a penalty. A double therefore should not be passed without a trick or two unless you have no good suit to remove to. After a 5-level opening bid, again, the double merely shows a strong hand, and should be removed by your partner only if he has a good 6-card suit or better. This is the only practical way of dealing with such openings. Remember that you are unlikely to have the sort of trump holding with which to make a purely penalty double.

12. Penalty doubles

It is a curious fact that where every aspect of the game is accorded a detailed examination, doubling for penalties is discussed only in a cursory, even incidental, fashion. Curious, because there can be no more telling weapon in a bridge-player's armoury. Particularly at rubber bridge, knowing when to double is an invaluable asset. What you require is some knowledge, a pinch of psychology, and a generous helping of flair. Perhaps we cannot guarantee that the fish will always be there, but we hope we can give you some sound advice on the best tackle to use and the most likely water on which to cast your bait.

The first fundamental principle is that the odds we receive must be reasonable in proportion to the risk. Let us look at an absurd example: an inexperienced player, holding:

♠Q103 ♡7532 ◇964 ♣842

hears his opponents bid confidently to 7♠. He doubles on the basis that he has a sure trump trick if both top honours are on his right. Giving him the benefit of the doubt, let us say that this is about an even-money chance. Do you see why his double is preposterous? There are two reasons. Firstly, if his opponents are not vulnerable his double stands to gain an extra 50 points and lose 260 (210 for tricks and 50 for the insult). That means he is laying odds of 4-1 on this even-money shot. Secondly, if the distribution of the trump suit is this:

AJ874

Q103   2

K965

declarer will now make his contract when, without the double, he might well have played for the drop and been defeated – a turnover of no less than 1820 points! This brings us to our first rule: the possible gain must outweigh the possible loss.

It is a long time since S.J. Simon wrote his classic *Why You Lose At Bridge*. In his inimitable style, he castigated the folly of those who double a slam when they hold two aces. Of course, a lot of players have taken his point, but nevertheless there remain enough to give this hoary old chestnut one more turn over the brazier.

You double, Simon suggests, because you think they won't make it. But:

'How certain are you?'

'Pretty certain. I mean, I have got two aces. . . . But, of course, if one of them should be void . . .'

'Then they'll redouble, won't they?'

'I can't help it. It's unlucky. I had two aces, partner.'

The principle involved is only an extension of our first example: what do you stand to gain? Fifty miserable points – yet every time one of your precious aces is ruffed your double has cost you an extra 230 points . . . to say nothing of the occasions when opponents redouble (as good opponents often will) and your moment of self-indulgence has cost you 590 points. The next time you lay odds of nearly 11-1 on and it goes wrong, perhaps you will have the grace to blush.

Two lessons flow from this principle: that it is bad bridge to double for one down, and that it is even more imprudent to double at the risk of giving away valuable information. If your opponents bid to a confident 4♡, and you hold:

♠AQ74 ♡QJ109 ◇A74 ♣63

it would be very timid not to double. Yet with:

♠AQ74 ♡Q1072 ◇A74 ♣63

we would be very chary of doubling, particularly against good card-players. Don't forget the 'hidden loss' of a double in this situation. Left to discover the bad trump break for himself, declarer may often go down peacefully enough. If you forewarn him, this is what may happen:

Dealer South, Love All

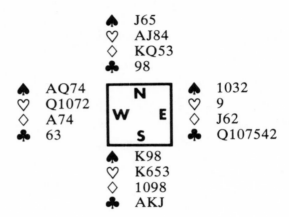

```
                    ♠  J65
                    ♡  AJ84
                    ◇  KQ53
                    ♣  98
   ♠  AQ74                        ♠  1032
   ♡  Q1072          N            ♡  9
   ◇  A74         W     E         ◇  J62
   ♣  63             S            ♣  Q107542
                    ♠  K98
                    ♡  K653
                    ◇  1098
                    ♣  AKJ
```

You lead ◇A and continue the suit (any other defence is worse). Declarer cashes his ♡K, notes the fall of East's 9, and proceeds to finesse the 8. Reasoning that you are likely to hold ♠A, he continues by finessing the ♣J. There are no more problems. Now you can see what your double has done.

In an uncontested auction, it is generally a mistake to double confident bidding. But when the opposition fumbles its way into an eventual contract, an apparently dangerous double can sometimes yield a surprising harvest. In order to clarify this we must examine some common bidding sequences to make sure that we can recognize the 'ring of confidence' when we hear it. Obviously when an opponent has made a forcing bid, they may well have reserves of strength. Less certain is a sequence such as 1NT-3NT, or 1♠-4♠ – in the first case the responder might have considerable reserves, as might the opener in the second. Contrast these auctions with the two shown below, in which *both opponents are limited.*

> (a) 1♠-2♣   (b) 1♠-2♣
>   2♠-2NT   2♠-3♠
>   3NT   4♠

In the first sequence, the opener has limited his hand with 2♠, and his partner has corrected with a non-forcing 2NT. In the second sequence the responder has issued a very mild invitation over his partner's limited 2♠. If you have a promising-looking double, such sequences are ideal for you. One word of warning: do not double opponents on the bidding if they do not understand what they are doing. They don't give you your money back, or even understand your reproachful glare.

This was a particularly poignant illustration of the principle stated above. Sitting South at pairs, one of the authors held:

♠974   ♡KJ8   ◇AQ65   ♣K103

and was gratified to hear the following unopposed East-West sequence: East 1♡, West 1♠, East 2◇, West 2♡, East 2NT, West 3NT. With both opponents apparently stretching beyond the limit, and every card offside, a double was automatic and full of promise. Alas, West held

♠KQJ83   ♡Q94   ◇J7   ♣Q95

and declarer made ten tricks without breathing hard.

Now, let us suppose you hold:

♠KJ765   ♡A5   ◇J103   ♣J103

and the bidding has gone:

South	North
1♠	2◇
2♠	3♣
3◇	3♠
4♠	No

Do you double or not?

As a child you were taught not to answer a question with a question . . . but that is precisely what you should do here: '*Am I East or West?*' If you are West, sitting over declarer, this is a sound double on the principles we have just studied. If you are East, sitting under declarer, you may well find that declarer will pick up your trumps with the ease of a gymnast tying his shoelace. This brings us to a third important question: do the cards lie well or badly for declarer? As an illustration, here is an extreme example. The hand occurred many years ago: North-South were highly competent players, East was an expert, and West was a worthy if somewhat pompous stockbroker.

Dealer North, Game All

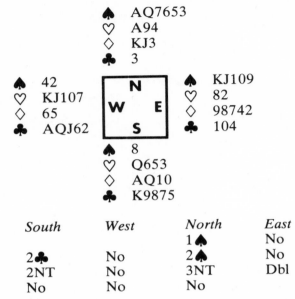

	♠	AQ7653
	♡	A94
	◇	KJ3
	♣	3

West		East	
♠ 42		♠	KJ109
♡ KJ107		♡	82
◇ 65		◇	98742
♣ AQJ62		♣	104

	♠	8
	♡	Q653
	◇	AQ10
	♣	K9875

South	West	North	East
		1♠	No
2♣	No	2♠	No
2NT	No	3NT	Dbl
No	No	No	

South misjudged the play and emerged with only five tricks. But it wasn't North-South who screamed in the post-mortem – it was West! 'How dare you double with only 4 points . . . might have landed us in the soup . . . jolly lucky I had a good hand!' It wasn't too difficult for East to apologize as he wrote down +1100 on his score-sheet.

The next consideration to be borne in mind is, 'Have they got a better spot?' Usually players with a bit of experience are inclined to be too apprehensive. With an uninterrupted sequence it is rare to find opponents discarding a 5-4 fit for an adventure with only 5 trumps between them. That is not to say that grotesque misunderstandings never occur – they do, but usually only when there has been aggressive intervention, or a misunderstanding of what was intended to be a cue-bid. Without postulating a hard-and-fast rule, we suggest that if opponents exchange a reasonable amount of information before settling in a contract which you feel sure is doomed, you should double. Very often they will stand their ground, and equally often they will retreat into another strain, to meet an even more devastating fusillade from your partner. Here is a typical example:

Dealer South, Love All

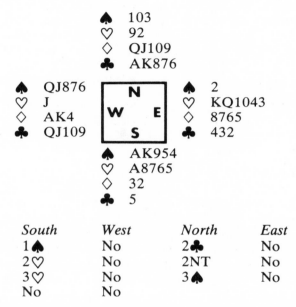

	♠ 103	
	♥ 92	
	◇ QJ109	
	♣ AK876	

♠ QJ876		♠ 2
♥ J		♥ KQ1043
◇ AK4		◇ 8765
♣ QJ109		♣ 432

	♠ AK954	
	♥ A8765	
	◇ 32	
	♣ 5	

South	West	North	East
1♠	No	2♣	No
2♥	No	2NT	No
3♥	No	3♠	No
No	No		

West's failure to double was pathetic, and his excuse ('I was afraid they would run to 4♥') even more so.

To conclude our examination of doubles based solely on the opponents' bidding, imagine that the exchanges start with an opening 4♠ on your right. You hold one of the two hands shown below – which is the sounder double?

(a) ♠AK32	(b) ♠KJ108
♥KQ2	♥AJ9
◇J763	◇762
♣109	♣753

The answer illustrates an important principle – the theory of the Unpleasant Surprise. When you hold hand (a) you should remind yourself that your opponent knew quite well that he was missing the AK of trumps when he bid. To double would be quite unsound. Hand (b) is an entirely different kettle of fish: declarer has apparently chanced his arm with a broken suit such as AQ97654 or AQ976543. Finding KJ108 stacked over him will come as a nasty shock, for which he has made no provision.

The following hand is a happy memory from some years ago. West held:

♠J10987 ♡432 ◇109 ♣653

and heard his opponents bid as follows:

South	North
1♠	2◇
2♠	3♠
4♣	

At this point West doubled. Yes, with only 1 point. Observe that both opponents are limited: with AKQ and 5 small trumps between the two hands they are doubtless counting on losing no trump trick, whereas you know they are certain to lose two. East, who had two aces, not to mention other goodies, could not help asking how West managed to find a double. 'You did well to stick it,' came the dead-pan reply.

13. Co-operative doubles

So far in our examination of penalty doubles we have studied only the principles that apply when opponents have monopolized the bidding. When your own side has also taken an active part, further considerations apply. This is the moment to nail what can be one of the most dangerous fallacies ever to pervade the minds of honest, decent players – the 'co-operative double'. The propaganda for this cultured form of hara-kiri is disseminated by bridge writers who should know better. This is the kind of thing they dangle in front of their innocent readers:

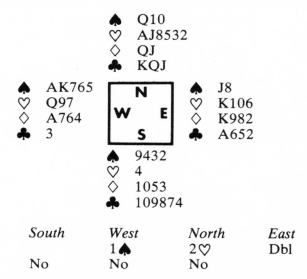

```
                    ♠ Q10
                    ♡ AJ8532
                    ◇ QJ
                    ♣ KQJ
  ♠ AK765                        ♠ J8
  ♡ Q97          ┌─────────┐     ♡ K106
  ◇ A764         │    N    │     ◇ K982
  ♣ 3            │ W     E │     ♣ A652
                 │    S    │
                 └─────────┘
                    ♠ 9432
                    ♡ 4
                    ◇ 1053
                    ♣ 109874
```

South	West	North	East
	1♠	2♡	Dbl
No	No	No	

The defence starts with two rounds of spades and follows with the Ace of Clubs and a club ruff. Ace and King of Diamonds and another club ruff leaves West on lead to play a spade. Declarer ruffs and East over-ruffs. The defence has now taken the first eight tricks. When East plays a club and West ruffs with the Queen there is no way that declarer can avoid losing two more tricks. Five down. Very pretty. Most impressive. But let us change the hand a little so that it looks like this:

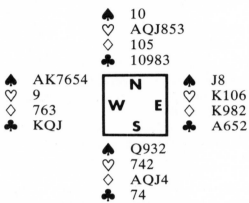

Now you can't break 2♡ with a pick-axe. Don't tell us that with this hand West should remove the double – from his point of view he has the same three likely defensive tricks as before. After one or two such disastrous 'co-operative doubles' you may find that every time you have an ordinary sound penalty double your wretched partner is going to remove it.

Does this mean we should set our hearts firmly against all co-operative doubles? No: subject to certain safeguards they are no more dangerous than catherine-wheels on Guy Fawkes' night. These then are the essential pre-requisites for a sound co-operative double:

(i) The possible gain must outweigh the potential loss. In this context it is clearly necessary to be more wary of doubling, say, 2♡ than two of a minor, because if this double misfires you have presented your opponents with a game.
(ii) There must be no attractive alternative. Always exhaust the possibilities in your own strain before attempting to chastise the opponents.

(iii) The context of the bidding must make it crystal clear that this is a double made in the expectation that partner will use his judgement.

The East hand in the examples shown fails all three tests. In terms of gain and loss, East cannot reasonably expect to pick up more than 500 with his double (the enticing 1400 of the first example requires a miracle fit and some keen defence), while he is risking the loss of 670 – the rubber at rubber bridge, a zero at match-points, a massive swing in the i.m.p. game. There is a perfectly sound alternative available in a bid of 2NT; and the bidding situation is a routine one for a common-or-garden penalty double based on powerful trumps and a misfit for partner's suit.

Here is another hand to consider in the light of our second principle:

♠K765 ♡KQ96 ◇743 ♣82

You hold those cards as East, and the bidding goes:

South	West	North	East
	1♠	2♡	?

It would be premature (to say the least) to double here. You are not sure to beat 2♡, you might make 4♠ your way, and for all you know you may shortly be given a chance to double 3♡. It is all very well being quick on the trigger, but results are more satisfactory when the gun is loaded. For the present you should bid 2♠, and await developments.

Obviously the most complex of our three principles is the third. Suppose you hold this hand as East:

♠1098 ♡KJ6 ◇A872 ♣1042

and the bidding has gone:

South	West	North	East
	1♠	2♡	2♠
No	No	3♡	?

To double now is 100% correct. East has given an excellent picture of his assets, and it should be easy for West to judge whether to stand the double or retreat to 3♠. East has shown his spade support (thus enabling West to judge that he will not make many defensive tricks with, say, AKxxxx), and has also limited his defensive prospects by failing to double 2♡. Note that this double closely resembles some of the types of competitive double discussed earlier, and indeed the two varieties are often hard to distinguish. Normally a double after both sides have agreed a suit comes under the heading of a 'game-try double', but this can hardly be the case here – East could only bid 2♠ on the first round, and West could not proceed, so clearly East cannot hope for a game and is simply saying that he has a maximum raise with some defence and is sure that his side can do better than allow North to play in 3♡ undoubled.

It is not only the doubler who must display sound judgement – his partner also has a vital role to play. The occasions when your 'main enemy' removes a double that would have produced a telephone number only just outnumber the times when he accepts a double with a defenceless hand. Once upon a time, players were taught not to open the bidding unless they had two defensive tricks; then came the apostles of Acol, preaching that it was good tactical sense to get in the first blow. As with many *avant-garde* theories, this one has a lot to be said for it provided that it is not carried to excess. Consider your next bid on the hands below after the bidding has started:

South	West	North	East
1♠	2♡	Dbl	No
?			

(a) ♠AK765   (b) ♠KQJ987 (c) ♠AKQJ98 (d) ♠K9872
    ♡10   ♡10   ♡10   ♡Q42
    ◇A743   ◇KQ43   ◇K43   ◇AQJ2
    ♣1098   ♣QJ   ♣A73   ♣3

With hand (a) you have reason to be well satisfied with the course events have taken: your opening bid was dubious because of the ungainly 2♠ rebid you would have had to make over a 2♡ response, and your hand with its three quick tricks is well suited to defence. A pass is clear cut.

Hand (b) contains too many secondary honours, and the spades are unlikely to play a significant role in the defence. Remove to 2♠.

With hand (c) you have at least two defensive tricks, but here it must be doubtful whether the penalty you will collect is going to justify missing a probable game. At equal or unfavourable vulnerability the correct action now is to take a punt at 3NT; only at favourable vulnerability would it be correct to stand the double.

Hand (d) was not much of an opening, but there are two factors which should influence your decision now: first, you have three trumps and a singleton; secondly, you have no attractive rebid if you do decide to disturb the double. A pass here is mandatory.

Playing with a good partner, you should normally accept a double unless your defensive values are substantially less than he will reasonably expect. That phrase is the key: we do not suggest that you should refrain from opening on hands with less than two defensive tricks, merely that you should bear in mind that partner will *expect* you to have that much defence. Remember that he knows the score as well as you do, and will not make hazardous doubles which could result in making the other side a present of a game. It is most disruptive of partnership confidence to establish a pattern of swingeing doubles striking nothing but the night air.

In the hurly-burly of rubber bridge it is essential to be philosophical about the disasters which will inevitably occur from time to time. Yet even after twenty years of stoical imperturbability one type of idiocy remains hard to bear. This is the miserable concept that no double at the level of one is sufficiently lucrative. Provided that the double is sound in the first place, there are excellent grounds for electing to defend such contracts. Remember that players who are suitably cautious with their two-level overcalls are quite prone to make risky overcalls at the one level. And when we say 'players' we include such great players as the Italian Blue Team, winners of so many World Championships. The members of this team deliberately pursued a policy of making aggressive one-level overcalls to disrupt their opponents' constructive bidding, and until the development of Sputnik doubles this policy was spectacularly successful. For several reasons, such 'unsound' overcalls will very often emerge unscathed – all the more reason to make sure they are punished heavily when the chance is there.

It is usually bad bridge teaching to say 'always' or 'never'. Yet for all practical purposes we suggest that you should never make a penalty double of a one-level contract without five trumps, and that you should be more than wary of standing such a double from partner if you are void in trumps. In this context the difference between a void and a singleton is often of immense significance, as very often the killing defence lies in an immediate attack on declarer's trumps. Here is an instructive example:

Dealer West, Game All

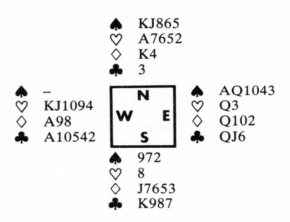

```
                  ♠  KJ865
                  ♡  A7652
                  ◇  K4
                  ♣  3
      ♠  —                      ♠  AQ1043
      ♡  KJ1094      N          ♡  Q3
      ◇  A98       W   E        ◇  Q102
      ♣  A10542      S          ♣  QJ6
                  ♠  972
                  ♡  8
                  ◇  J7653
                  ♣  K987
```

The bidding goes:

South	West	North	East
	1♡	1♠	Dbl
No	No(?)	No	

East leads the Queen of Hearts, which declarer wins, continuing with a small heart ruffed by dummy's 2 of Spades. When declarer plays a diamond from table, West wins with the Ace and, having no attractive switch, continues the suit. In with the King of Diamonds declarer plays a heart. Appreciating that his miserable partner has no trumps, East does the best he can by ruffing in with the 10 of spades and continuing with the Ace and another, killing dummy's trumps and establishing a two-trick set – not really adequate compensation for giving up a vulnerable game. Observe the difference if you give West one of dummy's small trumps, and dummy a second heart: now declarer is probably limited to three tricks, as West will fire his trump through declarer as soon as he gets the lead.

To conclude this chapter, we switch the spotlight to another situation in which good players reap a regular harvest from smooth co-operation and partnership understanding. This is when an opening suit bid has been followed by a take-out double and a redouble. We have already covered the essentials of this position in Chapter 4: if the opener passes the redouble he is encouraging his partner to double the escape bid for penalties, and if he then removes this double he is saying that though his hand is strong in high cards he thinks it will pay better to search for game than to penalize opponents in the particular strain they have chosen. We now concentrate on the occasions (the majority) when taking a penalty looks promising.

As a guideline, the redoubler should not double the escape with fewer than four cards in the suit. But often he will be able to *suggest* a penalty by passing. For example, suppose you hold as South:

♠J4　♡AQ42　◇Q107　♣Q1043

and the bidding goes:

South	West	North	East
		1♠	Dbl
Rdbl	No	No	2◇
No			

Remember that the redoubler is assumed to be short in his partner's suit. South's pass here is a clear invitation to North to find a penalty double if he has three or more diamonds and no attractive alternative bid.

It is a well established principle that if the opener disturbs the redouble without waiting to hear the escape bid he is weak and unsuited to defence. So what action should you take if you hold this hand as North:

♠AQ987　♡4　◇KQ104　♣1097

and the bidding goes:

South	West	North	East
No	No	1♠	Dbl
Rdbl	No	2◊	2♡
Dbl	No	?	

Should you stand it? Assuredly! You have already warned your partner that you are minimum, and probably little interested in defending against a heart contract (the most likely refuge for the enemy after a take-out double of a 1♠ opening). In the context of the bidding you have no reason whatever to be ashamed of your hand – after all, you opened third in hand, which you might well have done with less. Yet how often does one hear the pathetic bleat, 'I couldn't stand it, partner – I didn't really have an opening and you had already passed. . . .'

14. Lead-directing doubles

In principle, you should double to protect your rightful due on a hand, not to profit from the carelessness or poor judgement of your opponents. For example, if your opponents bid up to 3NT and you are looking at 17 points or so, it may be tempting to double on the simple arithmetic – they cannot have the normal high-card requirement for their contract. However, such a double is unsound in theory, for a number of reasons. First, opponents may have a long suit to run giving them nine or even more tricks off the top; secondly your double will place the outstanding strength in your hand and may enable declarer to make an 'impossible' contract by means of end-plays, squeezes and other such instruments of torture. But the third and best reason is that if you keep quiet and defeat the contract, you have your good result already. Your partner is marked with a virtual Yarborough – ask him after the hand whether he is satisfied with 100 points or so from the undoubled defeat.

For these reasons, a double of a freely bid game or slam is liberated for conventional use, and is so used by all good players. It has the effect of alerting your partner to the fact that you think the contract may be defeated on one particular lead. There is a great deal of divergence of opinion about some of the finer shades of meaning of lead-directing doubles, but what we describe in this chapter is the normal practice among experts.

A. DOUBLES AT THE GAME LEVEL

If you double a contract of 3NT after your partner has bid a suit, the double confirms that he should lead that suit. Such confirmation may well be essential: your partner may be reluctant to lead away from tenace holdings in a suit in which he has made an overcall. Two or three cards to an honour in partner's suit and some values outside justify a double to ensure that partner does not settle for some more passive opening lead.

When you yourself have bid a suit, the meaning of the double is more controversial. Standard practice has long been that such a double calls for the lead of the suit you have bid, and this interpretation is clearly useful when you have opened 1 ◇ on:

♠A6 ♡84 ◇KQJ1063 ♣QJ8

and your opponents insolently sail into 3NT. Clearly it is reassuring to be able to make certain that partner leads his unpromising singleton 2 of diamonds, rather than an imaginative and disastrous spade from three small.

However, although this method is still the most commonly employed, on grounds of frequency some experts have taken to reversing the meaning of a double in this situation. After all, partner is likely to lead your suit anyway unless he has a really promising alternative. There are many situations when you wish you had never bid at all, because partner is going to lead your suit when you can be almost sure that a different lead will beat the contract. The increasingly popular theory, which we endorse, is that in these circumstances you should double and hope partner can work out which lead you want. Here are two examples; in each case you sit South:

(a) ♠J8532 ♡KQJ10 ◇AJ6 ♣A

South	West	North	East
1♠	3♣	No	3♠
No	3NT	No	No
?			

It is certainly reassuring here to be able to double to stop partner leading your tattered spade suit. Even if partner is not able to read the situation and decides to lead a diamond, you are still more likely to break the contract than with a spade lead; and most of the time he will be able to judge which lead you do want.

(b) ♠AK742 ♡64 ◇AJ109 ♣75

South	West	North	East
1♠	No	No	Dbl
No	2NT	No	3♣
No	3NT	No	No
?			

You cannot be sure of defeating this contract even with a diamond lead, but this surely holds out more hope than a spade – West has a couple of spade tricks on this bidding. Here you could have doubled 3♣ if it was a club lead you wanted, so a double from you now will give partner a choice between the red suits, and quite often he will choose right.

When your side has not bid at all, doubles 'out of the blue' are almost always lead directing. Fairly well known is the rule that a double of 3NT calls for the lead of dummy's suit, and this is generally sound . . . but you should listen to the bidding, look at your own hand, and be prepared to over-ride this traditional interpretation when judgement suggests. For example, what does East want West to lead after this bidding:

South	West	North	East
1◇	No	1♠	No
3◇	No	3♡	No
3NT	No	No	Dbl
No	No	No	

Does he want a spade or a heart? Don't bother to poll this hand for opinions – you are likely to get a 50-50 split of the vote. Perhaps a spade is a little more likely, as East could presumably have doubled 3♡ if his hearts are all that good – but then again he might have been afraid to drive opponents into a better 4♠ contract. The best answer for West is to look at his own hand; most of the time he will be able to guess right with confidence, so that the bid can in effect be used in two senses. Try these two hands, as West, in the context of that auction:

(a) ♠84
    ♡K1062
    ◇Q63
    ♣J1062

(b) ♠Q952
    ♡J98
    ◇A7
    ♣8762

With hand (a) the spade lead is obviously right. On hand (b) you are surprisingly strong in both majors, but with North presumably holding five spades it is very unlikely that your partner has enough there to suggest a deadly attack, and you should lead a heart – the Jack will be the most helpful card.

Sometimes the double may not call for a lead at all. How about this?

South	West	North	East
1♣	No	1♠	No
3♣	No	3NT	No
No	Dbl	No	No
No			

The opener has shown a 6-card suit, which makes it very unlikely that West expects a club to be the killer. More likely he has clubs well guarded and senses a misfit. His hand may be something like this:

♠9 ♡QJ1073 ◇AQ7 ♣KJ98

He is strong enough to be sure the opponents do not have more than a point or two in reserve, so the double is safe enough and reasonably certain to produce a fair profit. Note that even here a club lead may turn out best, though it is not essential.

One obvious possibility is that you have a void, or perhaps a singleton with a certain trump entry. Again, you may be able to judge that partner has a singleton – for instance, if you have 4 cards in a suit opponents have bid and supported. Left to himself, he may not relish that lead.

A double of a suit game does not call for any particular lead, though it does generally seek to direct partner's attention towards a particular line of defence. When the auction is limited you may well wish to double simply because you know the cards are lying badly for declarer and that he will get an unpleasant surprise or two. There is nothing to stop you making this sort of straightforward penalty double. But there are some situations where the double comes as a complete surprise, and in this case your partner should try to divine the meaning of the double before he leads. Here is an example of a contract defeated by such a double:

Dealer North, Love All

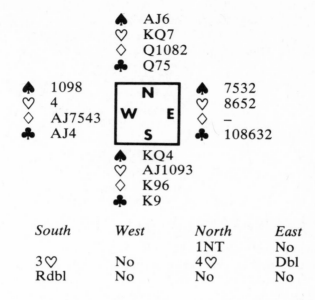

♠ AJ6
♥ KQ7
♦ Q1082
♣ Q75

♠ 1098
♥ 4
♦ AJ7543
♣ AJ4

♠ 7532
♥ 8652
♦ —
♣ 108632

♠ KQ4
♥ AJ1093
♦ K96
♣ K9

South	West	North	East
		1NT	No
3♥	No	4♥	Dbl
Rdbl	No	No	No

That was how the bidding went in one room in a team-of-four match. East's double could fairly be described as imaginative, and one pictures him turning pale green at the sound of the redouble, but in the end all was well: West rightly concluded that the out-of-the-blue double was based (as often) on a void, and started off with the Ace of Diamonds, followed by the 3 as a standard suit-preference signal for a club return. The two ruffs defeated a contract which would have made with ease on the routine spade lead.

And what can the meaning of a double be in a situation like this?

South	West	North	East
1NT	No	3NT	Dbl

Again opponents are unlimited, in that North may well have more than the minimum for his game raise; East is simply saying that he believes there is a lead which will defeat the contract. What that lead will be is for West to deduce. There are always some helpful clues – East's big suit is likely to be the one in which West himself is shortest, and since opponents have made no effort to investigate prospects in the major suits, East is more likely to hold a solid major than a solid minor. Hands on which East should chance a double after the auction shown are:

(a)	♠AKQJ7	(b)	♠KQJ1062	(c)	♠QJ10984
	♡532		♡10732		♡QJ7
	◇64		◇A		◇A4
	♣J84		♣J3		♣A3

You will find that an intelligent partner will almost always be able to find the lead you want. Whether that lead will in fact beat the contract is another matter, of course!

B.   DOUBLES AT THE SLAM LEVEL

The idea of lead-directing doubles of slam contracts is attributed to Theodore Lightner, a contemporary of Ely Culbertson. The theory of such doubles merges closely with the common-sense meanings attached to game-level doubles which we discussed in the previous section. However, as the 'Lightner Double' was born as a convention rather than an expert 'treatment', the subject is more clearly defined. Briefly, the double of a freely (as opposed to sacrificially) bid slam calls for an 'unusual' lead. This specifically excludes any suit bid by the defence, any unbid suit, and trumps. The usual reason for the double is possession of a void, often in dummy's main suit but occasionally in one of declarer's suits. For example, after this bidding:

South	West	North	East
1♡	No	2♠	No
3♡	No	4♣	No
6♣	Dbl	No	No
No			

what should East lead? A major, certainly, but which? The traditional answer is a heart, dummy's bid suit, but the modern school will tell you to look at your own hand and decide for yourself in which suit partner is likely to be void:

(a) ♠J54   (b) ♠Q96432
    ♡J86543   ♡A5
    ◇QJ10   ◇QJ10
    ♣6   ♣64

With hand (a) you should lead a heart; with hand (b) the obvious shot is the Queen of Spades, a suit-preference signal asking for a heart return.

When opponents have reached a slam after a contested auction, you may wish to let your partner know that your defensive tricks lie outside the suit you have called. After the bidding:

South	West	North	East
4♡	4♠	No	6♠

it would be reasonable to double with:

♠– ♡QJ1096532 ◇AK ♣632

However, you must be reasonably certain that if you get the lead you want you are going to beat the contract; it would be foolhardy to double with:

♠75 ♡KJ1096532 ◇A7 ♣6

as there is no reason to suppose that your side has a second defensive trick.

A double of a no-trump slam when there is no clear indication of a lead (for example, when opponents have bid no suits) generally alerts partner to the fact that you have the contract defeated in top tricks – you may have two aces, or, more likely, a suit head by AK. There is no certainty that partner will lead the right suit, but he is more likely to strike gold if he knows there is some to be struck.

C. DOUBLES OF ARTIFICIAL BIDS AND CUE-BIDS

The extensive use of conventional bids in the modern game enables the defending side to pass snippets of information about their values in suits bid artificially by their opponents. The double of such a bid can have two distinct meanings, and it is very important to be able to distinguish between them. The double may be employed to suggest a sacrifice or it may suggest a lead. The simplest approach to this potentially complex subject is to discuss first those situations in which it is practical to consider a sacrifice, and treat the remaining possibilities as lead-directing.

Doubles at a low level (for example, when opponents are in a game-forcing situation) and all doubles of artificial bids on the first two rounds of the auction should be played as showing tricks in that suit and interest in a possible sacrifice. Common cases are doubles of an opening 2♣ and the 2◇ negative, or asking bids and the conventional responses to them.

A low-level double of a conventional bid which is not game-forcing and may even be weak, such as a Stayman 2♣ or a low-level transfer over 1NT, may be used in a constructive sense. This is a matter for partnership agreement, but the most common approach is to double merely to show strong competitive values without reference to any particular suit. This in fact fits in with the normal rules for take-out doubles.

At higher levels, or after the second round of the auction, it is normal to double artificial bids in order to suggest a lead. This means you need defensive tricks in the suit, not necessarily length. This type of double occurs after cue-bids and artificial responses to Blackwood or similar high-level conventions. To double a Blackwood response of 5◇ with QJ109xx in the suit is a popular and utterly futile gambit. Not only will it incite partner to make a lead which will surely be unproductive, whatever his holding in diamonds, but there is another disadvantage which is often forgotten: when you double an artificial bid you give your opponents at least one and possibly two (if they redouble) extra rounds of bidding, which they may find invaluable for exchanging sufficient extra information to be sure of their final destination. Before venturing a double in such cases, always ask yourself which side is likely to benefit more.

Here are three examples with relevant bidding:

(a)   ♠97   ♡KJ1064   ◇742   ♣K73

South	West	North	East
1♣	No	2♠	No
3♠	No	4◇	No
4♡	?		

(b) ♠AQ5 ♡75432 ◇6 ♣8632

South	West	North	East
2NT	No	3◇	No
4◇	No	4NT	No
5♠	?		

(c) ♠KQ73 ♡65 ◇Q752 ♣J84

South	West	North	East
		1♡	No
2♣	No	3♣	No
3♡	No	4◇	No
4♠	?		

On hands (a) and (b) it is reasonable to double to suggest a lead, but on hand (c) it would be very unwise. First because you cannot even be sure that your partner is going to *be* on lead against the final contract; secondly because you are not sure that a spade lead will necessarily be best; and thirdly because opponents may be able to make a control-showing redouble and so gain extra space in the auction.

There is sometimes a useful negative inference to be drawn from your partner's failure to make a lead-directing double when he had the opportunity. For example; suppose you hold:

♠J96 ♡753 ◇842 ♣8632

and the bidding goes:

South	West	North	East
		1♣	No
2♠	No	3♠	No
4NT	No	5♡	No
6♠	No	No	No

Clearly you have no reason to doubt your opponents' belief that they can make a slam on this hand; indeed, you may even be grateful that they have stopped in a mere six. Still, you have to lead something – what?

Some players when faced with such a problem will stare at the ceiling for a few minutes trying to find inspiration for a brilliant attack; others will shrug hopelessly and lead the card nearest their thumb; but the thoughtful player will reflect that if a club lead is the killer partner could have suggested it with a Lightner double, whereas a heart lead could have been demanded by doubling the Blackwood response. Of course there is no reason whatever to expect a diamond lead to defeat the contract, but it is the one lead that your partner has had no chance to suggest.

It is that sort of tiny edge that makes the expert.

Before leaving the subject of doubling artificial bids, we have to consider the meaning of a redouble of such a double.

We start with the simplest case: the redouble of a double of a cue-bid. This is generally agreed to be showing second-round control in the suit. As was hinted at earlier, injudicious doubles of cue-bids give the cue-bidding side extra space to exchange information. Two unwise doubles of this kind enabled an expert pair to bid a grand slam with precision on this deal from match-play.

Dealer West, N-S Game

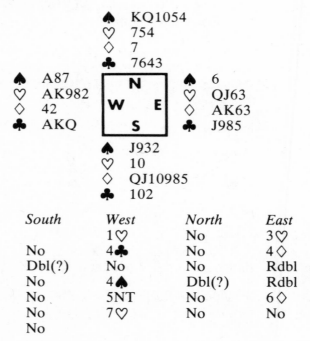

	♠	KQ1054
	♡	754
	◇	7
	♣	7643

♠ A87		♠ 6
♡ AK982		♡ QJ63
◇ 42		◇ AK63
♣ AKQ		♣ J985

	♠	J932
	♡	10
	◇	QJ10985
	♣	102

South	West	North	East
	1♡	No	3♡
No	4♣	No	4◇
Dbl(?)	No	No	Rdbl
No	4♠	Dbl(?)	Rdbl
No	5NT	No	6◇
No	7♡	No	No
No			

South's double of 4 ◇ was pointless – he knows a sacrifice at this vulnerability is not likely to be a success, and has no reason to assume a diamond lead against 6 ♡ will achieve anything. Similarly, North's double of 4 ♠ is futile – it is going to be his own lead, and again he cannot be interested in a sacrifice. (In case our readers have any doubts on this score, 7 ♠ doubled costs 2,300 on normal defence, a poor investment to save 1510.) East profited from the opportunity to show his second-round controls in the two suits by redoubling, and use of the modified Grand Slam Force located the Queen of Hearts, to reassure West that all the gaps were indeed stopped. If North-South remain silent, West will not be able to learn about the trump queen *and* the second-round spade control, and the big fish may get away.

There is one case in which it is recommended that the redouble should show *first*-round control, and that is when the cue-bid was a general purpose one in opponents' suit, not necessarily promising control at all. For example, you hold as West:

♠A7 ♡KQ953 ◇J6 ♣AJ54

and the bidding goes:

South	West	North	East
	1 ♡	No	2 ♣
2 ♠	3 ♣	No	3 ♠
Dbl			

East's 3 ♠ bid is presumably a no-trump probe, and without the double you would have to bid 3NT, aware that it might well play better from partner's hand. The helpful double gives you the comfortable option of redoubling to show the Ace, and if partner holds, as he well may, something like:

♠Q6 ♡J4 ◇AQ6 ♣KQ8732

the incautious double may have saved you from a nasty accident.

A redouble of a high-level artificial bid, such as the response to a Blackwood inquiry, is again control-showing. In this case, the redouble should promise the best control not yet shown – that is, if first-round control has already been shown by one partner the redouble shows second-round control.

When the double is of a low-level artificial bid, and purports to show strength in the suit doubled, a redouble indicates a desire to play in the redoubled contract. In this sequence, for instance:

South	West	North	East
1NT	No	2♣	Dbl
Rdbl			

South is showing good clubs, and suggesting that 2♣ redoubled may be a playable spot if his partner's hand is suitable. If North's Stayman inquiry was based on:

♠AQ75 ♡K9 ◇A842 ♣753

he should have no qualms about passing the redouble, which should surely be the easiest route to a big score.

15. The psychology of the double

It is strange how even good players fail to address their minds to the considerations that arise from the varying standard of opposition they are likely to encounter, especially at rubber bridge. Here is a case in point: East-West are game and 60 up:

West	East
♠AQ9642	♠K84
♡J	♡K1096
◇KQ42	◇A3
♣AJ	♣10942

South	West	North	East
	1♠	No	2♠
Dbl	No	3♡	Dbl
No	3♠(?)	No	No
No			

Of course 3♠ was easily made, for game and rubber. But 3♡ doubled would have yielded at least 700, possibly 900. Bad enough in any circumstances . . . but East and West were experts playing against uninspired opposition, and in such a case the 3♠ bid is horrific. West should have been delighted to have even a 300 penalty in the bank and then continue the fight at odds of 3-1 on (or even better, remembering the part-score), with a first-class partner against inferior opposition.

In general terms, it comes to this: if you consider your side to be distinctly superior, you should welcome the chance to stand a penalty double. If on the other hand you feel outgunned, let the fairy gold pass you by – bid your games, clinch the rubber, and hope to cut against a weaker pair next time. Of course, some players never feel outgunned – if you are one of those we can only wish you well and hope you are on good terms with your bank manager.

Players weaned on duplicate tend to be a little hazy about the odds at rubber bridge. At duplicate, if opponents are vulnerable and you are not, it is a fine result to save a game at the cost of 300 points, and you still show a profit if you lose 500. At rubber bridge, 300 is no bargain and 500 is a disaster. Why the difference? Well, at rubber bridge, once your opponents have clinched the first game it is 3-1 against your winning the rubber. If you then save for 300, it is still 3-1 against . . . and the rubber is going to cost you 3 units more if you do lose it. If (like North-South in the example above) you have a part-score against you, then the odds are even worse.

But, you say, you might make a slam on the next hand? Yes, but so might your opponents . . . and theirs is worth more than yours! There is no possible mathematical justification for saving in such cases – it is a blind gamble at very poor odds.

Next consider the very different case when neither side has a game. Now to save a game at the cost of 500 is a small loss at i.m.p. and a total disaster at pairs; yet at rubber bridge it does not seem to us to be too high a price to pay to continue the rubber at evens instead of 3-1 against, especially if the opposition are weaker than we are.

Another curious fallacy that persists even among quite good rubber-bridge players is that it is dangerous to double opposition part-scores if partner's defence is suspect. They argue that if partner plays his usual sleepy game, a two-trick set may suddenly turn into 2♡ doubled and made. There are two answers to this. First, if you don't double your chances of emerging with a small adverse rubber are decreased. Secondly, if partner's defence is as bad as that, perhaps it is a good idea to get the rubber over! (A further point is that good opponents will notice that you are slow on the trigger, and will begin to take more and more liberties.)

Compared with rubber bridge, duplicate tends to be clinical, less emotional. We don't suggest that it is less exciting – only that the human factor is obviously less strong. The practised regular partnerships one encounters at the duplicate table will have

faith in each other's ability, and confidence in the interpreta-
tions they place on each other's bids. Let us look at an everyday
bidding sequence and consider how the psychological factor
works out in these two rather different worlds:

West	East
1♠	2♣
2NT	3♣
3NT	No

Let us suppose first that East-West are an experienced tournament partnership. What does this sequence mean? East's 3♣
bid says that his 2♣ was based on a goodish suit but substandard
high-card strength. West, knowing this, elects to bid 3NT anyway. Clearly he has some sort of club fit and hopes to bring in his
partner's long suit. Holding:

♠J1094   ♡72   ◇J103   ♣J1098

you know that the clubs will not run, and you have a good
double, especially if your reputation is that of a 'doubler on the
bidding'.

In the cut-and-thrust of rubber bridge it is essential to consider the ability of West. A bad player will often bid 3NT
because he doesn't recognize his partner's 3♣ bid as weak; an
even more dangerous type of player bids it because he likes
playing no-trump contracts and why the devil shouldn't he? In
these circumstances, you don't need much to double. There is an
element of poker in such doubles – it can pay against poor
opposition to double *even when you know they are going to make
it.* They will be inclined to trust you more than each other and
cut their own throats, either by retreating to 4♣ or by sticking it
out in 3NT and finding a way to go down by playing for non-
existent bad breaks.

There are many opportunities for the good psychologist at the
rubber-bridge table. For instance, everyone has met the rabid
protector. If an opening bid on his left is passed round to him, he
regards the situation as virtually forcing – simple *amour-propre*
dictates that he must reopen. We have many happy memories of
this philanthropist, such as this one:

Dealer North, E-W Game and 60, N-S 60

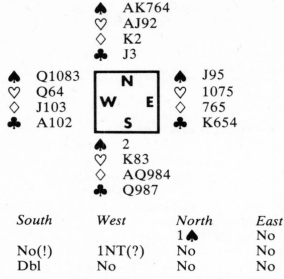

```
              ♠  AK764
              ♡  AJ92
              ◇  K2
              ♣  J3
♠  Q1083         N           ♠  J95
♡  Q64                       ♡  1075
◇  J103       W     E        ◇  765
♣  A102          S           ♣  K654
              ♠  2
              ♡  K83
              ◇  AQ984
              ♣  Q987
```

South	West	North	East
		1♠	No
No(!)	1NT(?)	No	No
Dbl	No	No	No

North found a heart lead, and declarer was held to two tricks. He was not very pleased, and nor for that matter was East, who had the impudence to suggest that his partner's call was ill judged. In the heated exchanges which followed no one bothered to work out that South might have scraped up a response to 1♠. . . .

With the flavour of poker still in the air, we come to the question of redoubles. As most elementary students know, there are three tests to determine whether a business redouble is a good proposition:

(1) Are we confident of success?
(2) Can we be sure of chastising the enemy sufficiently if they run?
(3) Are we possibly courting disaster if there is a really unpleasant distribution?

What is less generally known is that (1) is by no means the most important consideration – in our opinion, that distinction belongs to (3), closely followed by (2). Surely, you may say, there is not much sense in redoubling unless we are sure we are going to make the contract? Well, consider an everyday situation: As West you hold:

♠AQ109 ♡QJ1095 ◇3 ♣642

At Game All, the bidding goes:

South	West	North	East
1♣	No	1♡	1♠
4♡	4♠	Dbl	No
No	?		

Obviously you can hit them pretty hard if they run. Equally certainly, your good trumps should ensure that you cannot come to any serious harm in 4♠ redoubled. It is certainly possible that you might not have quite enough tricks . . . but we would redouble every time, except against opponents who regard retreat as a sign of cowardice incompatible with their well founded reputation for courage at all costs. This is not the time to punish *them*, but there should be many other opportunities for that pleasure.

When the bidding reaches the slam zone, psychological doubles can be particularly rewarding. This hand featured a fine performance by the East-West pair in a high-stake game at Crockford's in the early 1960s:

Dealer South, N-S Game

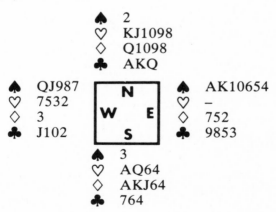

```
                    ♠  2
                    ♡  KJ1098
                    ◇  Q1098
                    ♣  AKQ
      ♠  QJ987                    ♠  AK10654
      ♡  7532           N         ♡  —
      ◇  3          W       E     ◇  752
      ♣  J102           S         ♣  9853
                    ♠  3
                    ♡  AQ64
                    ◇  AKJ64
                    ♣  764
```

South	West	North	East
1♢	No	2♡	2♠
3♡	5♢	6♢	Dbl
No	No	No	

It is hard to blame North-South for being bamboozled. West had a good idea that his partner might be void in hearts, and his 'void-showing' leap to 5♢ had the desired effect. Expecting West to be void in diamonds, North bid the slam in the wrong red suit. After East's Lightner double he might have had second thoughts, but even the greatest players can't see through the backs of the cards!

16. Doubling at I.M.P. scoring

I.M.P.s, or International Match Points, are used in competitions between two or more teams of four to reflect the difference between the scores obtained by two teams on the same hand. The difference between two scores is converted to I.M.P.s in accordance with an internationally agreed scale.

This method of scoring has a considerable effect on bidding tactics, especially where the penalty double is concerned. The main point is that the mathematical potential of every hand can be measured exactly. It depends entirely on the actual result, without reference to your partner, your opponents, or what has happened before. At rubber bridge, so much depends on preceding and succeeding hands (the latter obviously unknown quantities) that it is essential to be possessed of nice judgement even if the potential of the hand is known. Assume, for example, that you could be certain that opponents' non-vulnerable sacrifice of 4♠ could be defeated by three tricks for a score of 500 points to you, but that your own hands could make 5♡, vulnerable, for +650. To double and accept the 500 is to submit to an absolute and calculable loss of 150 points, which converts to 4 I.M.P.s. At rubber bridge, however, there are other, non-mathematical factors that should influence your decision whether to double or not. How good is your partner? How weak are your opponents? Is the rubber going well or badly? All these points enter into a good player's calculations, and even when he has made his decision he has to wait until the end of the rubber to find out if he was 'right' or 'wrong'. To a certain extent this shows the different skills demanded by the two versions of the game: the only requirement at I.M.P.s is to be able to balance the probability that your side can make eleven tricks in hearts against the probability of taking six tricks in defence against a spade contract. Consider the simple calculation which follows:

If you double when 5♡ would make, you lose 150 points (4 I.M.P.s).

If you are defeated in 5♡ when a double would produce 500 points, you lose 600 points (12 I.M.P.s).

It is therefore clear that if your judgement (which we must assume to be accurate) tells you that you have a better than 75% chance of making eleven tricks, you should reject the penalty and try for the game.

Using the same method, let us examine a couple of other everyday decisions.

(1) You have the choice between accepting a 300-point sacrifice and trying for a non-vulnerable game. If you take the penalty when game is on, you have scored +300 instead of +420, for a loss of −120, or 3 I.M.P.s. If you bid the game and are defeated you lose 50 points instead of collecting 300, an overall loss of −350. You should therefore bid this game if the chances of success are more than 72%.

(2) The same position except that this time you are vulnerable. If you double (+300) when game is on (+620), you lose 320 points (8 I.M.P.s). If you are defeated in game (−100) instead of doubling (+300) you lose 400 points (9 I.M.P.s). Now it can be seen that it is sound policy to bid this game if the chances of success are 53% or better.

In fact it is always possible to calculate exactly the percentage below which a sacrifice should be accepted and above which the game (or slam) should be attempted.

Some of the figures may seem rather astounding at first sight. When opponents have found what you fear may be a very cheap sacrifice against your small-slam contract, you should contemplate calling a vulnerable grand slam with a percentage chance as low as 41½%. Without interference from opponents a grand slam should not be considered with less than about a 57% chance of success, but if the alternative is accepting a penalty of less than 1100 rather than being permitted to make an overtrick in six, then odds of less than 50% become acceptable.

Naturally, the exactness of the percentages quoted has little practical use (except perhaps to justify your decision in the post-mortem), but they do at least give a useful general guide in some situations. For example, as South, vulnerable against non-vulnerable opponents, you hold:

♠7 ♡AKQJ74 ◇QJ1095 ♣6

and the bidding goes:

South	West	North	East
		1NT(12-14)	2♣
3♡	3♠	4♣	4♠
4NT	No	5♠	No
6♡	6♠	No	No

Partner has found a forcing pass of 6♠, leaving the decision to you. At I.M.P.s you should bid 7♡, which is known to depend on the diamond finesse (partner must have at least two diamonds for his opening bid, and cannot hold the King as he has shown three aces and is limited to 14 points at most). The penalty from defending against 6♠ doubled is unlikely to exceed 700 points.

The following hand would present no problem to a rubber-bridge player, but at I.M.P. you are faced with a difficult though familiar dilemma. As South you hold:

♠K1086 ♡AQJ74 ◇A74 ♣6

You are vulnerable, opponents not, and the bidding goes:

South	West	North	East
1♡	No	3♡	3♠
?			

You would have bid 4♡ without the intervention, feeling pretty confident . . . but the game is no certainty, and you have now been offered the chance to take 300 or 500 instead. At rubber bridge, most successful players would accept the safe plus score to be had from doubling, reasoning that after this hand they will still be a game up, with some extra money in the bank. However, if the hand comes up in a match at I.M.P. scoring there are some other considerations to take into account. Each hand is now separate from previous and following hands, and you should concern yourself with the mathematics of the situation, and with tactical points that are unknown to the rubber-bridge pundit. First, consider the situation if your right-hand opponent had not made the 3♠ overcall, bearing in mind that it may be a thin one which will not be found in the other room. You would have bid 4♡, and whether this made or not the likelihood is that the result would be the same as at the other table. However, if your right-hand opponent really has a clear-cut 3♠ bid, you are unlikely to defeat it by the 700 points necessary to compensate you for the vulnerable game.

It now becomes a matter of straight arithmetic. If 3♠ is defeated by two tricks (+300) what odds are required to make it worth bidding on? Using the reasoning described above you will find that the answer is 53%. If the penalty from 3♠ is going to be 500, you should only turn down the offer if you reckon your chances are 80% or better. Say that you feel sure the penalty will amount to either 300 or 500, a reasonable assessment: now the odds required for game are 67%. The decision is close, but with the hand you hold the chances should be higher than that, and we recommend that you bid 4♡.

In cases where you have already bid to game and enemy action forces you to consider a 5-level contract, the same type of reasoning can be applied. Here is an example. As South, vulnerable against not, you hold:

♠A5 ♡KQ10964 ◇AJ64 ♣8

and the bidding goes:

South	West	North	East
		1NT	2♠
4♡	4♠	No	No
?			

The slight chances that opponents can make 4♠ doubled, or that it is a phantom, with your side unable to make 4♡, can both be discounted, so you can concern yourself merely with the chances of success in 5♡ as against the likely penalty from 4♠. As your partner did not double, the penalty is unlikely to exceed 500 points, and you may well finish up with only 300. If 500 points could be guaranteed, the odds required to bid 5♡ would be 75% or better. If only 300 points are expected, then a 53%

chance or more will be enough to bid on. This boils down to approximately 64% if you judge that the penalty will be either 300 or 500 points. An experienced player will consider that the chances of success in 5♡ should be at least 64%, and accordingly that is the best call at I.M.P.s, rejecting the sacrifice.

These examples serve to illustrate the general principle that at I.M.P.s you must be much less inclined to accept sacrifices than at the rubber-bridge table. Naturally this sometimes leads to reckless sacrificing by non-vulnerable opponents – you should not be deterred from applying the axe when you think you scent a penalty greater than the value of your missed game, or when you cannot see a very strong likelihood of making your higher contract. The greater the penalty you foresee, the higher the percentage chance required for a further advance in your own suit.

What about those annoying cases at low levels when you are tempted by the prospects of a large penalty which, again, may not compensate you for a possible missed game? Suppose you hold as South:

♠KJ96 ♡A7 ◇AQ64 ♣1085

You are vulnerable against non-vulnerable opponents and the bidding goes:

South	West	North	East
		1NT	2♠
		(12-14)	
?			

Surely this is Christmas? But is it? Since 3NT is reasonably sure to be made, for +600 or so, only a penalty of 700 or more will be adequate exchange. It is very difficult to hold declarer to only four tricks when he has a long suit, as he surely has here; although at rubber bridge you would certainly double, being well content with 500 points if you let a trick slip in defence, it is better at I.M.P. to reject the dangling carrot and go for the game.

Now change the South hand slightly to this:

♠KJ96 ♡87 ◇AQ64 ♣1085

The same conditions, the same bidding, and an entirely different proposition. You would not have entertained much hope of game without the 2♠ intervention, and though you now know that your spade honours are well placed and the lead is likely to be favourable it would be unrealistic to expect anything more than a part-score your way. A double here is obligatory.

When the vulnerability is unfavourable – that is, you are vulnerable and your opponents not – there will be many opportunities for resourceful opponents to make daring bids which pay off by restricting the penalty to 500 points when game is on for your side. After all, if your side can make nine tricks in no trumps, you can make 600 points by bidding 3NT, but only 500 by doubling 1NT. Equally, if you can make 12 tricks you can collect +1440 by bidding the slam, but only +1100 from doubling 1NT.

The semi-psychic Gardner or 'Comic' 1NT overcall, discussed in Chapter 1, at first presented no problems to the experts of the day. It seemed easy enough just to double with a strong hand and await developments. When the comedian rescued himself into his long suit, everyone at the table would know what was what. However, a top international player confronted with this situation had other ideas. He considered the possibility of standing the double of his comic 1NT and seeing what happened. He calculated as follows:

Tricks Made in 1NT	Loss	Opponents Can Make	Loss
0	1300	7NT	2220
1	1100	6NT	1400
2	900	5NT	660
3	700	4NT	630
4	500	3NT	600
5	300	2NT	120
6	100	1NT	90

Therefore by making no tricks, or only one, he would show a substantial profit; with four tricks, a small profit; with three or five tricks a small loss. If he made six tricks there would be no swing. So the only time his manoeuvre would misfire badly would be when he lost 900 points and held two tricks in defence.

Beyond the plain figures there is the fact that it is often difficult (especially in such circumstances) for the defence to take all the tricks available to them. We are well aware of the dangers of this approach, but one lesson emerges clearly. When your side is vulnerable and you have a game or slam on, you must not rely on doubled opponents to rescue themselves from doubles in order to assist your bidding. Consider this hand:

♠AK10987 ♡KQJ75 ◇– ♣K7

Your partner opens 1♡ and next hand overcalls 1♠. What now? A fantastic penalty is envisaged . . . but even if the 1♠ bidder is completely psychic and fails to take a trick at all, the 1300 penalty will not even compensate you for a small slam, much less the grand. It is better here to bid 3♠, agreeing hearts and showing spade control. The full hand was:

Dealer East, E-W Game

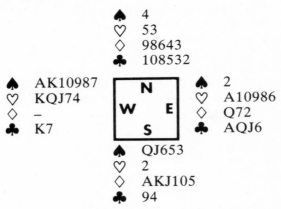

```
              ♠  4
              ♡  53
              ◇  98643
              ♣  108532
♠ AK10987              ♠ 2
♡ KQJ74     N          ♡ A10986
◇ –       W   E        ◇ Q72
♣ K7         S         ♣ AQJ6
              ♠  QJ653
              ♡  2
              ◇  AKJ105
              ♣  94
```

So 1♠ doubled would have produced no more than 700 points, and the grand slam in hearts was easy for East-West. The actual bidding sequence was good:

South	West	North	East
			1♡
1♠	3♠	No	4♣
No	4◇	No	4♠
No	5NT	No	6◇
No	7♡	No	No
No			

In I.M.P. play, close decisions whether to double or not may be affected by the state of the match. For example if you are well down in a team-of-four match it is often correct to seize the opportunity to gain points in a manner which would be unorthodox in any other situation. One common method of attempting to 'bring something in' is by doubling a little more readily, both for penalties and in competitive situations. For instance, if opponents bid to a game contract which you feel you can beat by one trick, or perhaps two at the outside, it is not normally winning tactics to double – you may have misjudged the position or, worse still, your double may guide declarer to an unlikely winning line of play. But if you feel that tamely accepting a flat board is not going to be enough to win you the match, you can be a little faster on the trigger. Similarly, a light intervention at low level may be justified when you are down, though at the beginning of the match you would have considered it unsound.

The converse situation is that if things have been going very well for you, you must do all that you can to prevent resourceful opponents from manufacturing a swing. It is dangerous to make speculative penalty doubles, and extremely foolish to make a risky intervention that may result in a large penalty.

Another factor that should sometimes be considered is the calibre of the two opponents occupying your seats at the other table. If you feel that they are likely to play an aggressive type of game, you should perhaps adopt similar tactics. In principle, if you feel that yours in the stronger team you should try to duplicate what you judge the other team will do. Paradoxically, it is when the other team is stronger that you should give more rein to your flair.

17. Match-point pairs

The scoring method used in match-point pairs competition is totally different from that found in any other form of the game, and this should affect your bidding to a very great extent. There are many situations where the decision whether or not to intervene or double is influenced entirely by the pairs scoring system. In most of them, the mathematical factors which apply relate to your estimate of the results your various actions will produce in relation to the results of other pairs holding the same cards. Bear in mind that, at pairs, your real opponents are not the two sitting at the table with you but all the pairs sitting at the other tables and holding your cards. This example shows the sort of decision that frequently arises in part-score battles at pairs. As South at Game All you hold:

♠K4 ♡AQ1074 ◇KQ74 ♣84

and the bidding goes:

South	West	North	East
1♡	No	2♡	No
No	Dbl	No	2NT
No	3♣	3♡	No
No	4♣	No	No
?			

At any other form of the game a double here would be out of the question. You may well reason that the most likely result is that you will beat 4♣ by one trick, but there is a far from negligible risk that it will be unbreakable and you will have doubled opponents into game. At pairs, you have to consider what will be happening over the rest of the field. Your opponents have shown considerable enterprise and daring in competing up to the 4-level after protecting, and this judgement is unlikely to be exercised by most of the field in an average pairs tournament. If they can make 4♣ you are going to get a very poor score indeed whether you double or not. If you defeat them undoubled and collect +100 you will still be well below average, as many other pairs your way will be scoring +140 in a heart contract. Bidding on in hearts is unthinkable: it is not impossible that 4♡ will be makable, but it is unlikely, and if you make a habit of allowing yourself to be pushed into game you do not want to bid you will show a huge loss on balance. The only chance of a good result is to double. This may easily have the effect of turning a below-average +100 into an excellent +200, or if things go wrong it will turn a near bottom of −130 into a complete bottom of −710. The difference in match-points between −130 and −710 is unlikely to be significant, but that between +100 and +200 will be very substantial.

It is an axiom of the pairs game that you should not allow your opponents to play unmolested in a part-score when your side has the balance of strength. This will normally result in a poor score whether you defeat the contract or not.

Here are some more examples of hands on which you would pass at rubber bridge but where more aggression is required at pairs. In each case you are South.

(a)   ♠Q64   ♡A653   ◇K1075   ♣J6

South	West	North	East
		1NT	2♠
?		(12-14)	

Double. Even beating the contract by two tricks undoubled is unlikely to be good, as your partner will probably make seven or eight tricks in no trumps. And a score of +50 is unlikely to earn you many match-points.

(b)   ♠QJ754   ♡3   ◇K62   ♣9543

South	West	North	East
	No	No	1♡
No	2♡	No	No
?			

Compete with 2♠. At other forms of the game it would be more prudent to pass, hoping opponents have misjudged by not bidding the game, but here that attitude will not do. Pairs who habitually push their opponents one higher on such hands reap big dividends over the year, scoring well on all the frequent occasions when eight tricks is the limit in hearts. With a similar shape but a little more defence, say:

(c) ♠A8754 ♡3 ◇K62 ♣J1043

a re-opening double would be a superior form of action, offering partner a choice of strains, and giving him the option of a smart penalty pass if he has, say, a near opening bid with good hearts and short spades. Such flirting with disaster would be unthinkable outside the strange world of pairs!

(d) ♠KJ75 ♡53 ◇K64 ♣7542

South	West	North	East
			1NT(12-14)
No	2♡	Dbl	No
2♠	3♡	No	No
?			

Here your side has the balance of strength, but East-West appear to have a heart fit and a double does not commend itself. It is better to call 3♠ rather than take the very considerable risk.

At the game or slam level doubles retain their normal meaning, usually a lead-directing one. A double for sheer profit when opponents have over-reached themselves, such as occasionally arises at rubber bridge or I.M.P. scoring, is rarely necessary at pairs, as defeating the enemy in their bad contract will give you a fine score. If they bid 3NT on a combined 21-count and go three down, you should get a top whether you have doubled or not. And sometimes they will have reached the correct contract by way of a crazy bidding sequence, in which case of course the double *will* produce a clear top . . . for them!

Vigorous competition at low levels is essential if you hope to win at match-point duplicate. We have already emphasized the need to compete freely when the points are more or less evenly divided. If you have a decent suit of your own you can bid it freely; if not, the low-level take-out double will often come in handy. You need not worry so much about the safety factor – it is more important to be constantly in the bidding even if, from time to time, you concede a penalty that you would not have risked at rubber bridge. On the hands below South should compete with a double rather than let the auction die:

(a) ♠KJ74 ♡7 ♢A642 ♣10743

South	West	North	East
			1♡
No	2♡	No	No

With this hand, you would certainly not be justified in reopening at any other form of the game – the prospect that partner may pass for penalties is a chilling one. At pairs, however, he should be alive to the possibility that you may be as weak as this, and if he does pass you should beat them – after all, you have a couple of defensive tricks, which is as much as you can be expected to produce.

(b) ♠KQ75 ♡K10863 ♢A5 ♣64

South	West	North	East
	1♢	No	1NT
No	2♣	No	3♣

Here it is more than possible that you do not have the balance of strength, but it is almost certain that 3♣, made or not, will not produce a good score for you. Partner is probably weak and fairly balanced – he will be unable to act if you do not.

(c) ♠AQJ75 ♡5 ♢KQ5 ♣J853

South	West	North	East
	1♢	No	1♡
1♠	2♡	No	No

Having correctly elected to bid your spades rather than doubling on the first round you are now well placed to give a good picture of your hand with a double, suggesting a sound overcall with good spades but some support for whichever minor partner cares to bid. Again, a penalty pass would not be particularly welcome, but that is a considerably smaller risk than passing.

In a pairs competition, a score of +110 or +140 will usually yield a good match-point score if the high cards are fairly evenly divided. As we have seen, it is correct to double in such cases when opponents have successfully done us out of our rights by aggressive competition. Nevertheless, this principle should not be carried too far. Suppose that you hold as South, vulnerable against not:

♠Q4 ♡AQ1086 ◇AJ94 ♣72

and the bidding goes

South	West	North	East
1♡	1♠	3♡	3♠
?			

Assuming that you would regard a double here as being for penalties rather than 'competitive', it would be over-bold to say the least to make such a double. For one thing, there is no guarantee that your side could have made 3♡, and you may already have done well by getting opponents to the 3-level. There is no reason to assume that the competition has been other than normal, and other pairs sitting your way may have been similarly inconvenienced. Defensive prospects are hardly enhanced by the doubleton Queen of opponents' suit. Finally, if the double is successful and you set them one trick, you have only turned +50 into +100, so that you still lose to all the 110s and 140s your way. This last point is one that should constantly be borne in mind: it is a better risk to make penalty doubles of this kind when opponents are vulnerable, because at least you get a top when it works. This knowledge is some compensation for the certainty that you are going to concede −730 or −670 from time to time!

The whole structure of match-point scoring alters the odds. At rubber bridge it is bad to bid a grand slam unless the odds are as good as 3-1 on; at pairs, a grand slam on a finesse is a fair proposition.

Let us look at an example of the same way of thinking as it applies to a routine decision whether or not to double. As South you hold:

♠KQJ92 ♡7 ◇J1098 ♣764

and the bidding has gone:

South	West	North	East
	1♡	No	1♠
No	1NT	No	3NT
No	No	No	

A double would of course call for a lead of dummy's bid suit, and that will no doubt give you a good chance of defeating the contract. At teams or rubber bridge it would be extremely rash to double, East being limited only by his failure to make a slam try. (If East had raised to 2NT and West had bid the third, the double would be a fair proposition.) But at pairs the double, even on this bidding, is a reasonable gamble. The spades are stacked, your partner can probably look after the hearts, and you will attract the best opening lead.

Another example of the same principle. As South you hold:

♠AJ109 ♡32 ◇876 ♣10987

and the bidding goes:

South	West	North	East
			1♠
No	4♠	No	No
?			

We have all met the player who doubles on this holding at rubber bridge; a fair description of such action is that it borders on the insane. But at pairs it is not too far-fetched to hope that North can contribute a couple of defensive tricks. Note that West is limited, and East has not made any move over 4♠.

After a poor start in a pairs competition, many partnerships try to recover some lost ground by frantic overbidding. In our experience this normally leads to a rapid descent to the bottom of the ladder. There are other, much better ways of trying for a par-beating result. Deliberate *under*bidding is often highly effective. The penalty double, too, can garner a valuable harvest of undeserved match-points: after all, if you push your way to 4♡ when the rest of the field is going to settle in 2♡ you are going to need a great deal of luck to get away with your gamble, but if you decide to make an unsound double of an enemy 4♠

contract you probably only need one extra trick to achieve your good result, and the double itself may induce declarer to take a losing line in the play. A spectacular example of this approach occurred in a recent county pairs event. On the last board of the tournament South held at Love All:

♠96   ♡J432   ◇8654   ♣J92

and the bidding went as follows:

South	West	North	East
	1♣	No	1♠
No	2♠	No	3◇
No	4♠	No	No
?			

It may seem a trifle eccentric to consider any action at this point, but South had calculated that a good board was needed to finish in the prize list, and that he was not going to get it by defending 4♠ undoubled. North is marked with some values, since West has limited his hand and East evidently did not feel able to go to game without some reassurance from his partner. It is a little surprising that North has not doubled, since he too knows the issues involved, but perhaps he is worried about helping declarer pick up the trumps. So South doubled, and found his partner with:

♠Q75   ♡AK9   ◇1032   ♣A854

The defence took their three winners early on, and declarer misguessed the Queen of Spades to go one down, North-South obtaining a cold top and second place in the final rankings. An irate East promptly called the director, claiming that South's double was 'frivolous and irresponsible'! Lucky, perhaps, but the thinking behind it was logical enough.

The calibre of a player's judgement is seen when the bidding reaches the game level and he is faced with a decision whether to bid one more (as a sacrifice or in hope of making it) or accept a penalty. Experienced players constantly score well in cases like this. At favourable vulnerability South holds:

♠Q104   ♡A765   ◇Q5   ♣J432

and the bidding goes:

South	West	North	East
	1♠	2♣	4♠
?			

Obviously 5♣ is unlikely to be makable, so the choice is between bidding it as a sacrifice and hoping to beat 4♠. Many players would reason that if they bid 5♣ they only need eight tricks to show a profit, losing 500 points instead of 620 for letting 4♠ make. But – and it is a big but – what if 4♠ isn't on? This is the classic 'bouncing' situation, where an astute East may be trying to play on your nerves by making a calculated overbid trying to drive you into a phantom sacrifice. The answer must to some extent be governed by individual style and temperament, and by knowledge of the quality of the opposition: if they lack the imagination to try this sort of acrobatic bluff, or if they are of the type that always bid one more in such situations, a bid of 5♣ will possibly pay off. But in most cases we would prefer a double of 4♠, with a pass as an unromantic but prudent alternative.

Pairs is a game in itself, and few players in the run-of-the-mill club event make sufficient allowance for the fact. In many cases their idea of 'pairs bidding' is to play in no trumps when they know something else would be better. The pairs who habitually finish at or near the top of the field owe their success to a proper understanding of the pairs factor in both play and bidding – and in bidding this means the constant application of pressure, never giving opponents a free ride, never letting them play in 2♡ when they can be pushed to 3♡, putting in lead-directing overcalls whenever half a chance arises, jamming their exchanges with thin pre-empts, and generally making their lives a misery.

We have already spoken of the artificial emphasis that pairs scoring imposes, yet pairs is a microcosm of bridge as a whole. As we write, strong Pass systems are in their infancy. They are not primarily designed to convey an extra degree of accuracy in constructive bidding, but rather to deprive their opponents of bidding space. Yes, that will surely be the strategy of the bridge wars of the future – a ceaseless assault upon the enemy's field of communication.